DATE DUE

~~FE 19 '97~~		
~~NO 16 '99~~		
~~DE 10 '98~~		
~~DE 18 '99~~		
~~JE 11 '01~~		
~~DE 18 '01~~		
~~JE 10 '02~~		
~~AUG 0 8 2002~~		
~~JY 27 '04~~		
NO 1 2 '09		

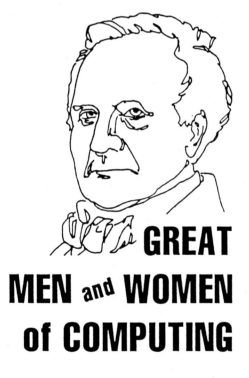

GREAT
MEN and WOMEN
of COMPUTING

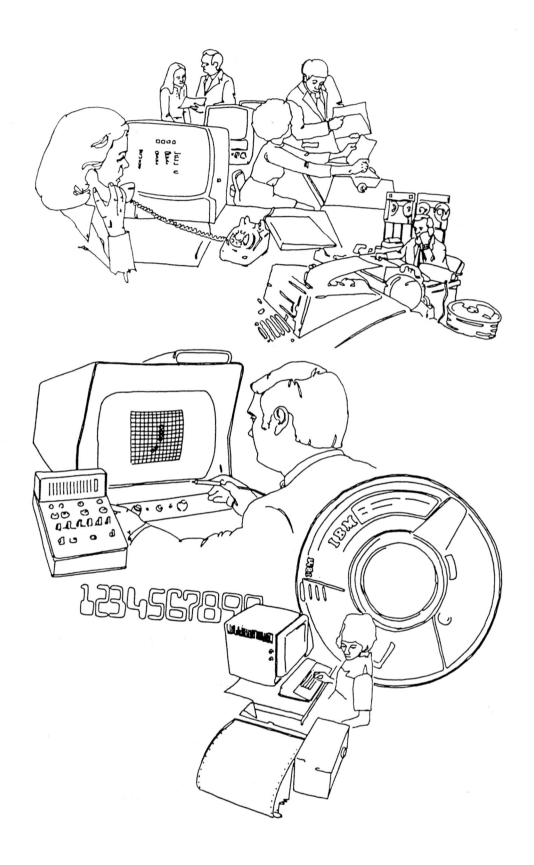

R

GREAT
MEN and WOMEN
of COMPUTING

Donald D. Spencer

CAMELOT PUBLISHING COMPANY
Ormond Beach, Florida

ACKNOWLEDGMENTS

the computer manufacturers, universities, encies who furnished the photographs for use in this book.

Printed in the United States of America

Printed on acid-free paper

Library of Congress Cataloging-in-Publication Data

Spencer, Donald D.
    Great men and women of computing / Donald D. Spencer.
        p.   cm.
    Includes bibliographical references and index.
    ISBN 0-89218-279-2 (alk. paper)
    1. Computers--Biography. 2. Computers--History. I. Title.
QA76.2.A2S64 1996
004' .092'2--dc20
[B]   95-44214
                                                       CIP

Published by
CAMELOT PUBLISHING COMPANY
P.O. Box 1357
Ormond Beach, FL 32175

PREFACE

Can you imagine what life must have been like in the days before computers were invented? We take for granted so many important computer-related discoveries that have made our lives richer, safer, more rewarding and more challenging. The computer was not discovered by accident. Rather it is the heritage of a dazzling procession of many great thinkers and scientists, extending over many centuries — people of profound wisdom and keen perception who devoted much time to the field of computing. We today — every one of us, at no cost to ourselves — are the beneficiaries of this rich heritage.

Who are these men and women to whom we owe this great debt? When did they live — what manner of people were they — and what was the exact contribution of each? They include, among the ancients, Pascal, who invented the first calculating machine; Charles Babbage, sometimes called the cranky grandfather of the modern computer; Augusta Ada Byron, the first programmer; George Boole, the inventor of *Boolean algebra* and one of the most influential thinkers of all time; Herman Hollerith who applied Jacquard's punched card principles to data processing. In modern times they include John Atanasoff, the inventor of the electronic digital computer; J. Presper Eckert and John Mauchly, developers of ENIAC, the first large-scale electronic digital computer; Grace Hopper, a pioneer in programming languages; John von Neumann, the genius behind the stored program computer; Seymour Cray, the developer of supercomputers; Thomas Watson, Sr., leader of the IBM empire; William Gates, the super developer of software for personal computers; John Kemeny; Niklaus Wirth; and others.

Illustrated with pictures and photographs, *Great Men and Women of Computing* is written in language stripped as far as possible of technical expressions. Thus, it will appeal to the lay reader, as well as to teachers, students and members of the computer profession, as a lively, concise and accurate review of the men and women involved in the evolution of the computer. Readers should link the present and future technology with that already encountered by the people in this book.

From that beginning when people used the abacus and "Napier's Bones" as primary calculating tools, this book traces the history of the computer through the discoveries of the many great men and women who took part in furthering this valuable calculating tool.

CONTENTS

GREAT
MEN and WOMEN
of COMPUTING

Two ways of computing in 1503—the counters and the numerals
(from Gregor Reisch: Margarita Philosophica; *Strassbourg, 1504).*

INVENTORS OF EARLY CALCULATING DEVICES

When people first began to use numbers, they knew only one way to work with them—counting. They counted the number of sheep in the flock, the number of animals they saw during a hunt, or the number of spears they owned. They used stones, sticks, shells, knots in a rope, notches on a stick, or marks in the sand to represent numbers. Clay tablets and papyrus scrolls were devised by prehistoric people for tallying and recordkeeping.

The absence or rarity of suitable writing material led to the use of the fingers as a way of representing numbers. From finger notation there developed an extensive use of finger computation. As society became more complicated, people had to develop fairly elaborate calculations involving subtraction, multiplication, and division that could not be done by finger computation only.

One of the earliest devices used to facilitate computations was the abacus. This reckoning board was particularly an instrument of merchants and tradespeople, and it could be applied universally, regardless of differences in languages and number systems. Although simple in appearance, in the hands of a skilled operator an abacus can be used for many computing needs. Even today, this calculating device is still used in several parts of the world.

The seventeenth century opened with developments of great importance to the art of computation. In 1614 John Napier, a Scottish politician, magician, and nobleman, published the first book of logarithms, which made it possible to find the product of two numbers without multiplication. Three years later he proceeded to devise a computing system based on logarithms—called Napier's bones.

Better techniques for keeping records by hand, along with specialized calculating devices, continued to be developed throughout the centuries.

In 1642 Blaise Pascal invented the Pascaline, an automatic desk-top machine that could add and subtract. In 1671 the German philosopher Gottfried Wilhelm Leibniz developed the "stepped reckoner." In this device, Leibniz overcame the defects of Pascal's toothed gears. A desk-top calculator like the Pascaline, the stepped reckoner could add and subtract automatically. It could also multiply and divide by using repeated additions and subtractions.

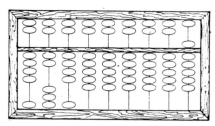

The first counting machine was undoubtedly the abacus. The abacus is an example of a digital computing device. It can be used for addition, subtraction, multiplication, and division.

JOHN NAPIER

1550-1617

The invention of logarithms by the Scottish mathematician, John Napier, provided science and mathematics with a vastly improved and rapid method of notation and calculation. Napier was born at Merchiston Castle, near Edinburgh, Scotland in 1550. At the age of 13, he entered the University of St. Andrews, but his stay appears to have been short, and he left without obtaining a degree. Little is known of his early life, but it is thought that he travelled abroad. Like other scientists of his day, he was caught up in religious controversies and wrote a notable work on the interpretation of the bible.

Napier spent his spare time on mathematics, and was burdened by the necessity of "multiplications, divisions, square and cubical expansions of great numbers," which took up a lot of time and were also "subject to many slippery errors."

In 1594 he conceived the idea that all numbers could be written in exponential form; 20 years later he published his logarithm tables. The word logarithm is from the Greek logos (reckoning, reason, ratio) and arithmos (number) and means the number of the ratio, or exponent. Napier's logarithm tables made an impact on the science of the day, something like computers are making on the science of our own time. Logarithms then, like the computers now, simplified routine calculations to an amazing extent and relieved working scientists of a large part of the noncreative mental drudgery to which they were subjected. Logarithms were meant to simplify calculations, especially multiplication, such as those needed in astronomy. Napier discovered that the basis for this computation was a relationship between an arithmetical progression—a sequence of numbers in which each number is obtained, following a geometric progression, from the one immediately preceding it by multiplying by a constant factor. Napier's invention of logarithms was comparable to other great inventions in relieving mankind of drudgery. Mathematicians, scientists, and astronomers in particular found their work incomparably easier.

Although Napier's invention of logarithms overshadows all his other mathematical work, he made other mathematical contributions. In 1617 he described methods of multiplying and dividing with the use of small rods known as Napier's bones. Napier's bones were simply a set of numbering rods upon which he transcribed the results of multiplication. All they did was free the user from memorizing the multiplication table. By arranging the rods side by side and matching up the numbers to be multiplied, the answer is quickly obtained with a minimum of computation. Napier's bones were described in one of Napier's papers, *Rabdologia*, published in 1617.

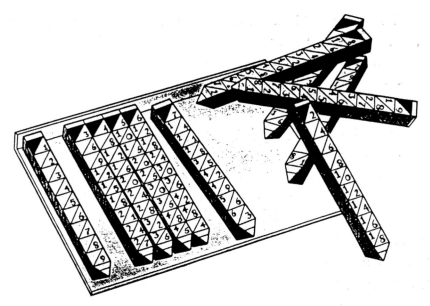

Napier's bones—a set of numbering rods made from slips of bones.

Napier's contribution must surely be considered a major milestone in humanity's struggle to improve methods of processing information. Before Napier's time the numerous scientific computations were done by tedious paper-and-pencil methods. Napier showed mathematicians how the more cumbersome operations of division and multiplication could be done by subtraction and division. His ideas, both in the theory of logarithms and in the use of computation rods, led directly to the invention of the slide rule some years after his death.

Napier died at Merchiston Castle, near Edinburgh on April 4, 1617.

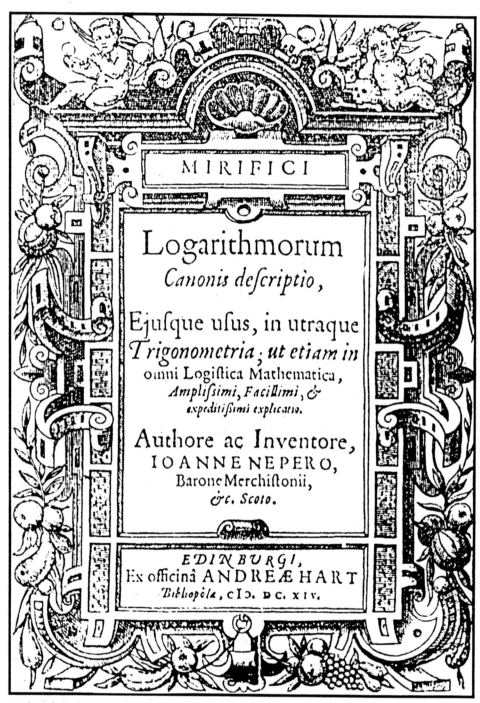

Napier's work on logarithms is contained in Mirifici Logarithmorum Canonis Descriptio. *The title page of this 1614 publication is shown.*

BLAISE PASCAL

1623-1662

Blaise Pascal was born on June 19, 1623, at Clermont-Ferrand, France. His mother died when he was three. He had two sisters, Gilberte, three years older, and Jacqueline, the baby. His father, Etienne, was a lawyer and mathematician. Etienne abandoned his career to raise Blaise and his equally talented sisters. The Pascal children's education took place informally, with Etienne introducing such topics as ancient languages but withholding subjects he felt were above the boy's head. He denied him, therefore, any books on mathematics. He even warned his friends never to mention mathematics in front of his son.

In the end, Blaise managed to beg from his father the most elementary definition of geometry, whereupon he taught himself its basic axioms, and succeeded, with no guidance whatever, in discovering for himself the first twenty-three propositions of Euclid in the correct order. This was enough to convince his father, who set about teaching him everything he knew about geometry.

When he was only sixteen, Pascal published a book on the geometry of the conic sections that for the first time carried the subject well beyond the point at which Apollonius had left it nearly nineteen centuries before. Descartes refused to believe that a sixteen-year-old could have written it.

Soon his father moved to Rouen, where he had been appointed tax commissioner. This job called for monumental calculations in figuring tax assessments. The man who had tried to hold back his son now turned to him for help in the thankless labor of hand-totaling endless columns of numbers. In 1642, when he was only 19, young Pascal had invented a calculating machine (called *Pascaline*) that, by means of cogged wheels, could add and subtract. The calculator could add a column of eight figures. He patented it and had hoped to profit from it, but did not. It was too expensive to build to be completely practical. Nevertheless, it was the first mechanical digital calculator able to do addition and subtraction. For many years Pascal kept improving his calculator, and made more than fifty models, trying to make his calculator handle fractions and square roots. His calculators were admired by the scientific community and made him famous in his time.

Pascal's calculator was a simple device about the size of a shoe box; however, it pointed out three principles that were used in later calculators: (1) that a "carry" could be accomplished automatically, (2) that subtraction could be accomplished by reversing

The Pascaline was a small box with eight dials (resembling telephone dials), each geared to a drum that displayed the digits in a register window. The machine marked a major step in the development of automatic computation because it had an auto "tens carrying" feature. The Pascaline could perform addition and subtraction. It was a commercial failure, however, because it was difficult to repair. In addition, clerks and accountants protested, fearing the loss of their jobs. The two dials on the extreme right of the machine were used for currency calculations and represent sous and deniers.

the turning of the dials, and (3) that multiplication could be performed by repeated addition.

In 1646, Pascal's interest moved toward physics. He demonstrated with the help of his brother-in-law that air pressure decreased with altitude as Torricelli had predicted, by taking a mercury barometer to the summit of Puy de Dome (a height of 1,200 meters, near Clermont-Ferrand). His interest in hydrostatics also led him to demonstrate that pressure exerted on a confined fluid is constant in all directions. This is called Pascal's principle and it is the basis of the hydraulic press, which Pascal described in theory.

In 1653, a friend, Chevalier de Mere, asked Pascal to solve some problems about dice. Pascal in turn wrote and began active correspondence with Pierre de Fermat. Together, Pascal and Fermat developed the first theory of probability. A year later he refined his generalized theory of numbers. He devised his arithmetic triangle from which Sir Isaac Newton deduced the binomial theorem and Gottfried Leibniz, the integral calculus.

In 1654, he had a narrow escape from death when the horses of his carriage ran away. He interpreted this as evidence of divine displeasure, and his conversion became sufficiently intense to cause him to devote the remainder of his short life to prayer and religious writings. He had given up science, mathematics, and technology, except for some work on the solution of the cycloid (undertaken to distract his mind from a toothache) and the promotion of a scheme for a public transportation system in Paris.

The last years of his life were dominated by illness and pain. He died at 39 on August 17, 1662. He was one of France's greatest mathematicians and philosophers.

GOTTFRIED WILHELM LEIBNIZ

(1646-1716)

Gottfried Wilhelm von Leibniz was born on July 1, 1646, in Leipzig, Germany, the son of a professor of moral philosophy at the University of Leipzig. Because the Leibniz family lived in a university community and were part of the academic circle, Gottfried was exposed to a scholarly environment early in life. His father's library was available to him, and before the age of 10, he had consumed books on the Romans, Plato, and the Greeks. He taught himself Latin, was soon reading Greek, and at age 14, was immersed in Aristotle. Years later, he was to admit that the ancient writers had a great effect on his understanding of the world's knowledge. He had learned to use words to attain clarity and to use them properly. There was no school in his day in which a boy of his genius could be educated; he was therefore left to the guidance of his own interests and he became self-taught.

At age fifteen, he entered the University of Leipzig as a law student; there he came in contact with the thought of men who had revolutionized science and philosophy, men such as Galileo, Francis Bacon, and René Descartes. He received a bachelor's degree at seventeen. At twenty, he received a doctorate in jurisprudence from Altdorf, and for 6 years thereafter pursued a career of law and diplomacy, attempting to stop Louis XIV's march on Holland. Although Leibniz never did get through to the king, he found it easy to gain favor with such figures as Christian Huygens, a leading physicist and mathematician. Huygens presented him with a copy of his mathematical essay on the pendulum. Gottfried quickly became impressed with the power of the mathematical approach, and Huygens became his mentor.

It was during this period that Leibniz became fascinated with mechanical contrivances. He was extremely impressed by the idea of a calculating machine and set out to study in detail the works of Blaise Pascal and Samuel Morland, and to construct a more perfect and efficient machine.

In 1671, he invented a calculating machine that could not only add and subtract, but could also laboriously multiply and divide. In 1694, he exhibited a working model of his calculator in London, and was made a member of the Royal Society, largely on the strength of his new invention. His calculator consisted of a series of stepped cylinders, each with nine teeth of different lengths. Smaller gears, each representing a digit of the multiplicand, were set above them and placed so each could be engaged by that number of the cylindrical gears' teeth. A complete turn of the set of long gears, therefore, registered the multiplicand once; the multiplier was expressed by the number of times the long gears were turned. Although the machine established many important principles to be used three centuries later in mechanical calculators, it was mechanically unreliable, like Pascal's machine, and unmarketable.

Late in 1675, Leibniz laid the foundations of both integral and differential calculus. For the process of integration, he proposed the familiar symbol ∫, an elongated "s" signifying "summation." Leibniz also introduced the symbol ∂ (for differentiation). Sir Isaac Newton had laid claim to inventing calculus in the 1660s, but Leibniz was apparently unaware of it.

In 1676, Leibniz left Paris for Hanover, where for the next 40 years he devoted his time to serving the Duke of Brunswick as historian, librarian, and chief advisor, and intermittently working on his calculating machines. Leibniz's later years were divorced from mathematical and scientific pursuits as he turned to philosophy. He developed the ingenious theory of monads—minute copies of the universe out of which everything in the universe is composed, as a sort of one-in-all, all-in-one. His last important contribution came in 1700 in Berlin, where Leibniz organized the Berlin Academy of Sciences and became its first president.

He died in Hanover on November 14, 1716, at the age of 70 during an attack of gout. His death aroused no interest in London or Berlin, and the only person present at his burial was his secretary.

Leibniz's calculator could not only add and subtract but could also multiply, divide, and extract square roots.

BOOLEAN ALGEBRA
AND DIGITAL LOGIC

George Boole, a nineteenth-century mathematician, introduced a theory of logic that was to prove very important to the development of electronic computers. Without going into the intricacies of what is now known as Boolean algebra, we can simply note that Boole reduced logic to two-valued *binary notation*. In binary notation, only the values 1 and 0 can be used to form numbers. By stringing enough 1s and 0s together, any number can be expressed—and with Boolean algebra, the numbers can also be operated on logically. Binary notation turned out to be virtually made to order for electronic components, which can be either on (the equivalent of 1) or off (the equivalent of 0).

BASE 2

OCTAL
DECIMAL
BINARY

GEORGE BOOLE

1815-1864

George Boole was born on November 2, 1815, in Lincoln, England, the son of a poor shoemaker. Boole attended only elementary school and a small commercial school before going out to work as an assistant teacher at the age of fifteen. He spent four years teaching at two different elementary schools. Coming from a stratum of society in which people were not expected to attend a university and, in fact, were discouraged from it, Boole had to educate himself entirely on his own. He was self-taught in mathematics and opened his own school in Lincoln when he was twenty. During scant leisure time, Boole read

27

mathematics journals in the Mechanics Institute, founded about that time for science education. There he wrestled with material written by mathematicians Isaac Newton, Pierre-Simon Laplace, and Joseph-Louis Lagrange, and began to solve advanced problems in algebra. His first paper, "The Theory of Analytical Transformation," was published in 1840 in the *Cambridge Mathematical Journal.* This paper and one published the following year, on the theory of linear transformations, were the precursors of the theory of invariance, without which there would have been no relativity theory. The papers impressed other mathematicians so much that they urged him to go to Cambridge. But Boole, now responsible for his aging parents turned the idea down.

In 1844, he discussed how methods of algebra and calculus may be combined in an important paper in the *Philosophical Transactions of the Royal Society.* The same year he was awarded a medal by the Royal Society for his contributions to analyses. Boole soon saw that his algebra could also be applied in logic.

In 1847, he published a pamphlet, *Mathematical Analysis of Logic, Being an Essay Towards a Calculus of Deductive Reasoning,* in which he argued persuasively that logic should be allied with mathematics, not philosophy. On the basis of his publications, Boole in 1849 was appointed professor of mathematics at Queen's College in Cork, Ireland (despite his lack of degrees), and for the first time experienced relative security. He remained at the college for the rest of his life.

In 1854 Boole published *An Investigation of the Laws of Thought, on Which Are Founded the Mathematical Theories of Logic and Probabilities.* This book, along with his 1847 publication, described his ideas and made him the father of modern symbolic logic. His logic, called Boolean algebra, was not realized until the latter part of the nineteenth century.

Boolean algebra is really an explanation of binary, zero-one logic. In the formula $x \cdot x = x$, the only numeric solutions in Boolean algebra are 0 and 1. If you represent a condition of no current flow in a circuit by 0 and a condition of current flow in the circuit by 1, then other Boolean formulas are possible:

$$1 + 1 = 1$$
$$0 + 1 = 1$$
$$0 + 0 = 0$$
$$1 \cdot 1 = 1$$
$$0 \cdot 1 = 0$$

Boolean algebra led to the design of electronic computers through the interpretation of Boolean combinations of sets as switching circuits.

Because Boole demonstrated that logic can be reduced to very simple algebraic systems, it was possible for Charles Babbage and his successors to design mechanical devices that could perform the necessary logical tasks.

The year after he wrote his *Laws of Thought*, he married Mary Everest, niece of Sir George Everest, for whom Mount Everest is named. The Booles had five daughters. The children were a testimonial to his ideas. His third daughter, Alice, made extraordinary mathematical discoveries without any formal mathematical training. The fourth, Lucy, also without any college education, became a lecturer in chemistry and head of the chemical laboratories at the London School of Medicine for Women. The youngest daughter published several novels and some music.

Boole died on December 8, 1864, after he persisted in lecturing after being caught in a bone-chilling rain, and so contracted a cold that turned into pneumonia.

Boole's name is a household word among computer scientists and mathematicians. His influence on the development of computers and their rules of operation was unique, and yet he is virtually unknown outside these fields.

George Boole

AN INVESTIGATION OF
THE LAWS OF THOUGHT
ON WHICH ARE FOUNDED
THE MATHEMATICAL
THEORIES OF LOGIC
AND PROBABILITIES

KEY-DRIVEN CALCULATORS

Blaise Pascal, Gottfried Leibniz and others entered numbers in their calculators by hand. Charles Babbage used hand entry in his Difference Engine, and went to punched cards for his Analytical Engine.

Would-be inventors soon sought some faster means of data entry and many of them thought of the use of depressible keys, such as actuated the piano. But this was a harder problem than it seemed. Two keyboard types of machines developed. In the key-driven type the energy to drive the machine was provided by the depression of the figure keys; in the key-setting type it was supplied by the depression of a handle after the figure keys were set. The difficulty with both types was that the actuating force was not constant and neither was its effect, and errors were probable.

In 1850 D.D. Parmelee got a patent for a key-driven adding machine. A number of key-driven machines were made between 1851 and 1887. Like Parmelee's, they could add only a single column of digits at a time. It was necessary to add the units first and note the total; then to clear the machine and add the carry figures to the next column. The competition to this type of machine was the trained human being, who was faster.

The next hurdle was to make the key-driven machine do what the machines of Pascal and Leibniz could do—add a number of columns, say six or eight, at the same time in a multiple-order machine.

In 1857, Thomas Hill got a patent on a multiple-order key-driven machine. In 1872, Robjohn patented a single-digit adding machine that did have a stop device to prevent overrotation of the units wheel, though there was nothing to prevent the overflow of the higher, or tens, wheels in the event of a carry. M. Bouchet made the first attempt to control the carried wheel in 1882, using a Geneva gear to lock the wheel. The Bouchet single-order machine was manufactured and some units were sold, but it never became popular.

By the end of the nineteenth century, mechanical calculators were in common use. In 1887, Dorr Felt formed a partnership with Robert Tarrant that produced the Comptometer, in which calculation was performed simply by pressing keys that actuated the number wheels of a register.

William Seward Burroughs invented the first commercially practical adding/listing machine in 1884. Burroughs' machine incorporated most of the features found in mechanical adding machines and made mechanized accounting a reality. He received a patent on this machine in 1888.

DORR FELT

1862-1930

Dorr Eugene Felt, an American machinist from Chicago designed an experimental multiple-order key-driven calculating machine. The machine was built from a wooden macaroni box and used keys made from meat skewers, key guides made from staples and rubber bands for springs. The important innovation is that calculation was performed simply by pressing keys, which actuated the number of wheels of a register. No setting of levers, turning of handles or other movements was required. This greatly speeded up the calculation process. Felt's first machine was known as the

Macaroni Box and was completed soon after New Year's day, 1885. Although it was a crude machine, Felt had hit upon the mechanical basis for the modern day calculator.

In 1886, Felt started to make mental versions of his calculator. This machine, called the Comptometer, was the first machine to have a full numeric keyboard. Felt had little money and he had to make the machines himself. In 1887, with Robert Tarrant of Chicago, he formed the Felt and Tarrant Manufacturing Company. Their Comptometer was to be a leader in the market for the next fifteen years. The value of this machine was enhanced by detailed instructions for the four basic operations and also for square and cube root, interest, discount, money exchange, and so forth.

Felt was also the inventor of the Comptograph, the first practical recording-adding machine. He was issued a patent on this machine on June 11, 1889. His first model was hand wound and could not print zeros. In following machines, each figure was visibly printed as the key was depressed. The paper was advanced by a hand lever which also activated the printing mechanism.

A young man by the name of William S. Burroughs became fascinated with the Felt machine and began to apply Felt's principles to his own inventive activities. In the end Burroughs produced a type of recording machine that proved to be more acceptable from an operative standpoint than the recorder made by Felt.

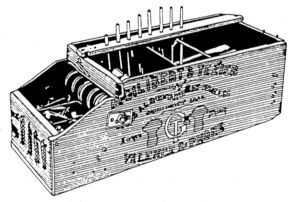

Felt's first calculator was a wooden model called the Macaroni Box.

WILLIAM BURROUGHS

1857-1898

William Seward Burroughs, an American bank clerk, was born January 28, 1855 in Rochester, New York. He acquired all of his schooling in the elementary schools. After a brief education he supported himself from the age of 15. When 20, he entered a bank in Auburn, New York. Analyzing his work, he found that about half his time was spent in trying to guard against error, half, of the remaining half in searching for errors made.

Burroughs' health gave way. Doctors said his only chance to live was to change his occupation. He then went to work in a machine shop in St. Louis. Often he worked far into the night conceiving a machine that would record amounts on paper, that would add these amounts just as recorded, without the slightest possibility of error, and would carry a progressive total just as fast as the amounts were listed, so that on pressing a key at any time a correct total would be printed instantly.

One day Burroughs was sent to repair some mechanism in a St. Louis dry goods store. His skill attracted a member of the firm, who learned of his ambition. This man interested other investors in the company Burroughs proposed to organize. Other money was obtained and Burroughs got room in a machine shop which did considerable experimental work for inventors.

Every dollar that Burroughs could scrape together went into his invention. He exhibited his first machine publicly in 1884. It formed the basis of his fundamental patent issued on August 21, 1888. It was the first ever granted for a key-set recording and adding machine. The basic principle of Burroughs' machine was the pivot. Leading mechanical engineers still declare this principle to be the soundest ever adopted for the purpose. Burroughs built with the idea that his machine must be as independent as possible of the human agency. He evidently had in mind the typist with her too-busy eraser, and decided at the start to do away with errors caused by accidentally striking the wrong keys. One safeguard he threw around his work was the "locked keyboard," a most ingenious idea which guarded against the possibility of the operator accidentally striking a wrong key after setting up the amount. This locked keyboard also made it possible for the operator to read the amount set up on the keyboard before printing it.

Although the machine was a success, he died before receiving much money for it. In 1905 the Burroughs Adding Machine Company was organized in Michigan as successor to the American Arithmometer Company. The company later became the Burroughs Corporation, one of the world's leading manufacturers of computer equipment, and today is part of Unisys Corporation.

A year before Burroughs' death he received the John Scott Medal of the Franklin Institute as an award for his invention. He died on September 15, 1895 in Citronelle, Alabama.

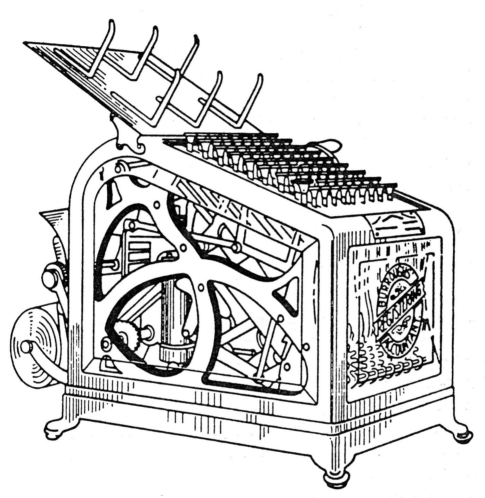

The first commercially practical adding/listing machine was invented in 1884 by William Burroughs. Burroughs' machine incorporated most of the features found in modern adding machines. With the introduction of this machine, mechanized accounting—initiated by Blaise Pascal—had become a reality.

SCIENTIFIC AMERICAN

A WEEKLY JOURNAL OF PRACTICAL INFORMATION, ART, SCIENCE, MECHANICS, CHEMISTRY, AND MANUFACTURES.

NEW YORK, AUGUST 30, 1890.

THE NEW CENSUS OF THE UNITED STATES—THE ELECTRICAL ENUMERATING MECHANISM.—[See page 137.]

PUNCHED CARD MACHINES

A major contribution to computing methods came from an unlikely source—the weaving industry. In 1801 Joseph Marie Jacquard developed an attachment for weaving looms that used punched cards to "program" a loom to create a specific pattern. The same pattern could be repeated many times, and exact copies of rugs and tapestries could be made.

However, it was not until the 1880s that someone thought of the punched card as a means for processing data. The occasion was a commercial problem that demanded a new computing method. The 1880 U.S. census had taken seven and a half years to count manually. By the time the returns were in, the census people were out in the streets collecting data for the next count.

Statistician Herman Hollerith solved the problem with machine readable cards and a corresponding machine to read the information on them. Hollerith's machines saved time and money.

JOSEPH MARIE JACQUARD

1752-1834

Joseph Marie Jacquard was born on July 7, 1752, in the village of Couzon, about three miles from Lyons in central France. Lyons, the second largest industrial city in France, hummed with the noise of silk looms. Both of Jacquard's parents worked in the weaving trade. His father, a weaver of gold- and silver-embroidered silks, and his mother, a pattern maker, were a modest, practical couple who believed in the virtues of thrift, loyalty, and hard work.

At the age of 10, Jacquard went to work as a "drawboy" in the weaving trade. Patterns were created in silk material by drawboys who lifted and returned the weighted vertical warp threads by hand. In later life, Jacquard became obsessed with eliminating the tedious function of the drawboy in silk manufacturing.

Jacquard invented the loom that made automatic weaving practical for the first time. Named the Jacquard loom after its inventor, it was the most important stage in the evolution of textile weaving by automating mass production methods. The Jacquard loom started a technological revolution in the textile industry and is the basis of the modern automatic loom. He first formed the idea for his loom in 1790, but his work was disrupted by the French Revolution, in which Jacquard fought on the Republican side. Jacquard returned to his loom design as soon as he was free to do so. At the Paris Exhibition of 1801, he demonstrated a new improved type of silk drawloom, and in 1805 he produced the Jacquard loom in its final form. It linked a system of punched cards with sprung needles that lifted only those threads corresponding to the punched pattern on the card. In this way it was possible to weave patterns of remarkable complexity in silk materials for table cloths, wall hangings, and bedspreads. In 1806 the loom was declared public property, and Jacquard was rewarded with a pension and a royalty on each machine.

The Jacquard loom aroused bitter hostility among the silk weavers, who feared that its introduction would deprive them of jobs. The weavers of Lyons not only burned machines that were put into production but attacked Jacquard as well. Eventually, the advantages of the loom brought about its general acceptance, and by 1812 there were 11,000 in use in France. In 1819, Jacquard was awarded a gold medal and the Cross of the Legion of Honour. His loom spread to England in the 1820s and from there achieved virtually worldwide use. By 1833, about 10,000 looms were in operation in England. In 1834 there were 30,000 looms in use in Lyons alone.

Charles Babbage admired a portrait of Jacquard. About 30 inches square, as precise as a line engraving, but made in beautiful colors, it had been woven in silk thread on a Jacquard loom, using some 24,000 cards. It inspired Babbage with the idea of "programming" his analytical engine by means of punched cards. Punched cards were also used by Herman Hollerith to feed data to his census machine.

Jacquard died on August 7, 1834, in Oullins, France, at the age of 82 with his mission completed. The drawboy had been replaced by an automated loom.

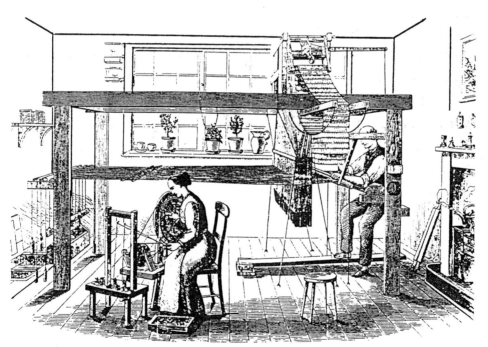

A Jacquard loom in use. The pattern of the weave is controlled by the belt of punched cards.

Twenty-four thousand separate cards were used for the self-portrait of Joseph Jacquard, woven in silk by a loom of his own design.

HERMAN HOLLERITH

1860-1929

Herman Hollerith was born in Buffalo, New York, on February 29, 1860, the son of a German immigrant couple. Immediately after graduating from the Columbia University's School of Mines in 1879, he became an assistant to one of his former teachers in the U.S. Census Bureau. During the next few years, he taught briefly at the Massachusetts Institute of Technology in Cambridge, experimented on air brakes, and worked for the patent office in Washington, D.C. During all of this time, Hollerith was occupied with the problem of automating the tabulation work of the census.

45

When the tenth decennial census was taken in 1880, the country had grown to fifty million people, and five years later the Census Bureau was still struggling to compile the results. It was not hard to foresee a situation where a given census would not be published before it was time to take the next one.

Hollerith, inspired by watching a conductor punch tickets with a basic description of each passenger, started work on a machine for mechanically tabulating population and other statistics. In 1884, he applied for his first patent on a machine for counting population statistics. He was eventually issued thirty-one patents.

Hollerith's most important innovations were the sensing of the holes through electrical contacts and the design of electrically operated mechanisms for incrementing the proper register in the tabulating machine. He also provided for one step in an electric sort. Each card was coded to fall into the proper pocket in a sorting box. From this point on, sorting had to be done by hand, but it was easier to sort punched cards than handwritten cards because the sorter could sight through the wanted hole or use a sorting needle. The card used in Hollerith's machine was 6.625 x 3.250 inches and had twenty-four columns, each with twelve punching places. Hollerith worked as an independent inventor, with no commitment from the census authorities to the use of his invention; however, he planned his system keeping in mind the requirements for tabulation of the population census.

In 1889, a committee was appointed to consider the means of tabulation to be used in the 1890 census. Three systems were tested, one of them Hollerith's. His system took only about two thirds as long as its nearest competitor to transcribe information. The commission estimated that on a basis of 65,000,000 population, the savings with the Hollerith apparatus would reach nearly $600,000. Hollerith's invention was adopted and an arrangement was entered into by the government with its inventor.

As a statistician and employee of the Census Bureau, Herman Hollerith proposed using punched cards in conjunction with electromechanical relays to accomplish simple additions and sortings needed in the 1890 census. Hollerith's Tabulating Machine enabled the U.S. Government to count the 1890 census twice as fast as the 1880 census even though the population had grown by 25 percent. The Hollerith concept, while improved upon through the years, remained the basis of the information processing industry through World War II.

Hollerith's Tabulating Machine—the first machine designed expressly for data processing. His machine handled punched cards at the rate of fifty to eighty per minute.

Hollerith subcontracted the development and construction of the keyboard punches to the Pratt and Whitney Company of Hartford, Connecticut, and of the tabulator to the Western Electric Company.

In 1890, three major events occurred in Hollerith's life: (1) he married the daughter of Dr. John Billings; (2) he received his doctor of philosophy degree from Columbia's School of Mines; (3) the United States conducted its eleventh census using his system. Dr. Billings was in charge of the work on vital statistics for both the 1880 and 1890 censuses, especially the collection and tabulation of data. While working at the Census Bureau, Billings, who was Hollerith's superior, also suggested to Hollerith that Jacquard-like punched cards might be the answer to the massive tabulation problems of the census.

In 1896, Hollerith formed the Tabulating Machine Company. Word of his success spread rapidly. Insurance companies used his machines for actuarial work, department stores used them for sales analysis, and the New York Central used them to keep track of their railroad cars. The Tabulating Machine Company became world famous.

Hollerith continued to modify and improve his machines, which were used for the 1900 census. In 1910, even though Hollerith had developed a system of hopper-fed machines that eliminated hand feeding of cards, he was unable to reach an agreement with the Census Bureau for their use.

When his Tabulating Machine Company became too large for individual control, Hollerith sold it. In 1911, the company became part of the Computing-Tabulating-Recording (C-T-R) Company. The C-T-R Company was a holding company and in 1924 was renamed the International Business Machines (IBM) Corporation.

On November 17, 1929, in Washington, D.C., a heart attack ended his life at the age of 69. What Henry Ford did for manufacturing, Herman Hollerith accomplished for data processing—a means for standardization and a format for the interchangeability of information.

5

DIFFERENTIAL ANALYZER

Another important development, which occurred between World War I and World War II, was the invention of the differential analyzer by Vannevar Bush at Massachusetts Institute of Technology. This machine was an assembly of gears, cams and differentials which simulated mechanically the various functions in a differential equation. When all were geared together, and the machine put into motion, the only solutions that could emerge were those which satisfied all the equation's requirements simultaneously. Analog machines like this, but rather simpler, were widely used in the Second World War for radar and gun operations.

VANNEVAR BUSH

1890-1974

Vannevar Bush was born March 11, 1890 in Everett, Massachusetts, a few miles north of Boston. One grandfather was captain of a whaler at twenty-one, the other was master of the first commercial craft ever to sail up the Amazon. His father, Richard Bush, left the sea to work his way through Tufts College, and later became a Universalist clergyman who served fifty years in Everett and nearby Chelsea.

After receiving bachelor's and master's degrees in engineering from Tufts College in 1913, he worked briefly at testing for the

General Electric Company, and then returned to Tufts to teach mathematics and electrical engineering. In 1916 he received a doctorate degree given jointly from Harvard University and the Massachusetts Institute of Technology.

While teaching, he also was involved with his inventions. One was the computing machine for solving differential equations. Its principal components perform the mathematical operation of integration. Bush and others at MIT invented the first continuous integraph, later called a differential analyzer, during the late 1920s. Its integrators consisted of replaceable shafts, gears, wheels, and discs and required much manual setting up. The analog computer operates electronically and faster (although not always as accurately) and accomplishes the same operations with components that take up less space. The first model of Bush's differential analyzer was completed in 1930. It was very, very big, and it was driven by a bunch of electric motors. Most important of all, it was general-purpose, which is to say that it could, with a bit of reorganization, be set to cope with more or less any problem where differential equations were involved. Bush was the first to introduce electronic components into a computing system, and as such the MIT differential analyzer represents a turning point in the history of computing.

Apart from the differential analyzer, Bush made significant contributions to various fields of science. He also had the knack of inspiring and fertilizing the minds of bright individuals who came into contact with him.

In 1940 he was appointed chairman of the National Defense Research Committee, which was responsible for co-ordinating scientific research to help the war effort. In this rule he wrote the report recommending the establishment of the Manhattan team, which eventually developed the atomic bomb.

After the war, he continued to serve on military policy committees and returned to his duties at the Carnegie Institution. He also prepared, at the President's request, recommendations on ways in which the wartime lessons could be applied to peace. The result was *Science: the Endless Frontier*, a report that urged heavy Federal support for basic research. The concept eventually was molded into the National Science Foundation.

Bush retired from Carnegie Institution in 1955 and returned to MIT where he remained until 1971. He was a member of scores of honorary and professional societies, and received numerous awards. In February 1970, with Dr. Conant and General Groves, he received the Atomic Pioneers Award from the U.S. Atomic Energy Commission.

In a career that spanned 60 years, Bush played many roles—engineer, teacher, inventor, author, businessman—but it was his skill as a forceful administrator that made him the logical choice to mobilize the scientists and engineers of the United States in 1940 as war threatened. He directed the work of some 30,000 people throughout the country, and had overall responsibility for developing such sophisticated new weapons as radar, the proximity fuse, fire-control mechanisms, amphibious vehicles, and ultimately the atomic bomb.

Bush died of a stroke on June 29, 1974 at his home in Belmont, Massachusetts. He was eight-four years old.

In the late 1920s Vannevar Bush was trying to solve equations associated with power failures. To handle such equations, he built, in 1930, the first automatic analog computer that was general enough to solve a wide variety of problems. He called his machine a "differential analyzer." The Bush differential analyzer originally gave its solutions in the form of curves; later it was adapted to have a five-register numerical output.

EARLY DIGITAL COMPUTERS

In the 17th, 18th and 19th centuries, scientific development centered around mathematics. Engineers, astronomers, and mathematicians all had extensive need for mathematical tables. These tables defined the relationship or difference between two numbers or sets of numbers and are the tools that scientists very early in time used to record their experiences so that others could benefit. Building these tables by hand was tedious and time consuming. A method of speeding up these calculations and freeing creative minds for more important work was an acute requirement.

An early 19th century English gentlemen and intellectual, Charles Babbage, was intrigued by the problem, and in 1812 conceived and designed what he called his Difference Engine. It was a relatively simple machine that could generate tables to an accuracy of six decimal places. In 1833, before the Difference Engine was completed,

Babbage designed another machine vastly more capable than his original device. He called the second machine his Analytical Engine, and spent the rest of his life and fortune refining but never completing it. Because of the concepts he incorporated in the Analytical Engine, Babbage is considered to be the grandfather of today's modern computer.

Not until the late 1930s, over 100 years after Babbage introduced his Analytical Engine, did work begin on the development of what are considered modern computers; this work was speeded by the pressures of World War II. The government saw the potential of these new computing devices in the war effort and funded their development handsomely.

In Germany, Konrad Zuse was working on relay calculators that incorporated the principles of binary arithmetic, a floating decimal point, and program control by punched tape.

George Stibitz, a mathematician at Bell Laboratories, developed a relay computer, called the Complex Number Calculator in 1939. A year later he used this machine to demonstrate remote computing.

In 1939, Howard Aiken of Harvard University began work on a machine to perform mathematical and scientific calculations faster. The Automatic Sequence Controlled Calculator (ASCC), which is also called the Harvard Mark I computer was completed in 1944.

CHARLES BABBAGE

1791-1871

Charles Babbage was born on December 26, 1791, in Teignmouth, Devonshire, England. From the very beginning, he showed a great desire to inquire into the causes of things that astonish children's minds. On receiving a new toy, Charles would ask, "Mamma, what is inside of it?" Then he would carefully proceed to dissect it and figure out how it was constructed and what made it work. All throughout his career, he continued to have a curious and questioning mind. This curiosity played a significant part in the development of many of his famous ideas.

He was one of the two surviving children of Benjamin Babbage, a wealthy banker, and Betty Plumleigh Teape, both descended from well-known Devonshire families. Babbage's parents were affluent and he had the opportunity to attend private schools.

After a succession of private tutors he entered Trinity College, Cambridge, in 1810. At Trinity College, Babbage's studies led him to a critical examination of the logarithmic tables used to make accurate calculations. He was well aware of the difficulty and tediousness of compiling the astronomical and nautical tables and dreamed of a machine that would one day calculate such tables. At Trinity College, he proved to be an undisciplined student, constantly puzzling his tutors. He was often annoyed to find that he knew more than his teachers. But in spite of his outward displays of rebellion, he was already on his way to absorbing the advanced theories of mathematics.

In 1815, Babbage, John Herschel, and other contemporaries founded the Analytic Society. Its purposes were to emphasize the abstract nature of algebra, to bring continental developments in mathematics to England, and to end the state of suspended animation in which British mathematics had remained since the death of Sir Isaac Newton.

After receiving his master of arts degree from Trinity College in 1817, Babbage plunged into a variety of activities and wrote notable papers on the theory of functions and on various topics in applied mathematics.

In 1822, Babbage designed his Difference Engine, considered to be the first automatic calculating machine. Based on the recommendation of the Royal Society, he was able to obtain a grant from the British government that permitted him to work on this machine. The Difference Engine was to be a special-purpose device, constructed for the task of preparing mathematical tables. After eight years of work, Babbage lost interest and abandoned this machine and turned to the design of the Analytical Engine.

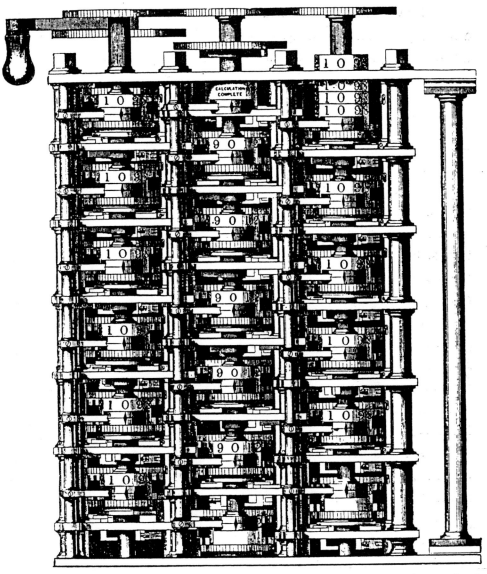

The idea for a Difference Engine that would compute mathematical tables, such as logarithms, was conceived by Charles Babbage in 1812. The engine was first announced by Babbage in 1822. The concept was brilliant; however, the assembly of the machine required parts with unheard-of precision. In 1832, Babbage lost interest in the Difference Engine and began working on his new machine. A model of the Difference Engine was built in 1859. It was adopted four years later by life insurance companies and was used for several years to compute actuarial tables.

In 1833, Babbage conceived his Analytical Engine, the first design for a universal automatic calculator. He worked on it with his own money until his death. Babbage's design had all the elements of a modern general-purpose digital computer, namely, memory, control, arithmetic unit, input, and output. The memory was to hold 1,000 words of fifty digits each, all in counting wheels. Control was to be by means of sequences of Jacquard punched cards. The very important ability to modify the course of a calculation according to the intermediate results obtained, now called conditional branching, was to be incorporated in the form of a procedure for skipping forward or backward a specified number of cards. The arithmetic unit, Babbage supposed, would perform addition or subtraction in one second while a 50 x 50 multiplication would take about 1 minute. Babbage spent many years developing a mechanical method of achieving simultaneous propagation of carries during addition to eliminate the need for fifty successive carry cycles. Input to the machine was to be by individual punched cards and manual setting of the memory counters. Output was to be punched cards or printed copy. Although Babbage prepared thousands of detailed drawings for his machine, only a few parts were ever completed.

The description of Babbage's ideas would not be adequate without mention of Augusta Ada Byron, Countess of Lovelace, who was acquainted with Babbage and his work. Her writings have helped us understand this work and contain the first descriptions of programming techniques.

An oversensitive and tactless person, Babbage was unpopular with many of his contemporaries. By the end of his life, he was disappointed by his failure to bring his principles within sight of completion; however, Babbage was actually attempting the impossible with the means at his disposal. He was a man born a hundred years ahead of his time. He died in London on October 18, 1871, surrounded by the drawings, cogwheels, and fragments of his hopeless, half-finished dream.

Babbage is thus the grandfather of the modern computer, and although this was not understood by his contemporaries, Babbage himself was probably aware of it.

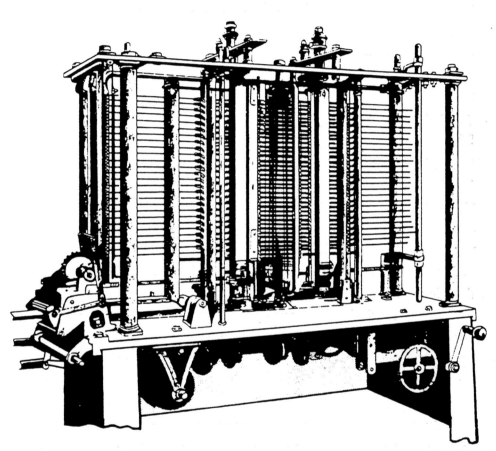

Charles Babbage devoted 37 years to perfecting a calculating machine, the Analytical Engine, which could be used to construct mathematical tables. While his project did not succeed, his underlying logic was sound and led to the modern day computer. Shown here is part of the Analytical Engine, based on Babbage's drawings and built after his death. This is the "mill" and printing mechanism, able to perform four arithmetical operations and print out the results to twenty-nine places.

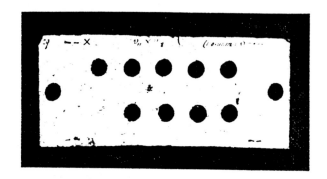

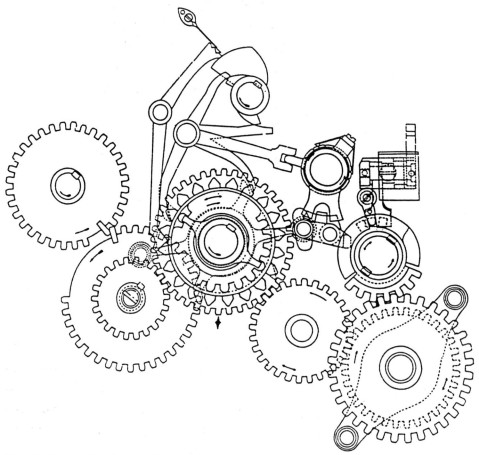

(Top) *A punched card designed by Babbage for his Analytical Engine. The punched cards used by Babbage were of two kinds—either to direct the nature of the mathematical operations being performed, or to select the variables.* (Bottom) *One of Babbage's drawings of part of his engine.*

KONRAD ZUSE

(1910-1995)

Konrad Zuse, born on June 22, 1910 in Berlin, Germany, studied construction engineering at the University of Berlin in Charlottenburg, and received his Ph.D. in 1935. He started his career as an engineer in the aircraft industry. He soon became aware of the tremendous number of monotonous calculations necessary for the analysis and design of static and other aircraft structures.

Pondering on methods for facilitating these time-consuming computations, he conceived of performing the calculations by machine. A computer machine, he reasoned as early as 1934, would have to be able to follow a sequence of simple computational steps, in which all variables and intermediate results would be named. Numbers would be entered from an input unit, and results would be placed in an output device. Internally there would have to be a memory , arithmetic unit, and a control section. Arithmetic would be performed in floating point, with separate units for the exponent and fraction. Numbers and instructions would be represented in the binary number system, and bistable switching units would be used. Zuse quit his job in the aircraft industry in 1936 to have more time to develop his ideas on program controlled computers. By 1937, working in his parent's apartment, he had hand-built a test model for a mechanical memory for sixteen 24-bit numbers. The Zuse Z1, completed in 1938, was completely mechanical, with a binary floating point arithmetic unit. The Z1 was an electro-mechanical relay computer with a very simple instruction repertoire, but it obeyed a punched paper tape program and was capable of logical decisions. The Z1 was built six years before the first American relay computer was built—the ASCC (Automatic Sequence Controlled Calculator) or Harvard Mark I. At this time German computer design was ahead of both American and British.

Drafted into the German army in 1939, Zuse worked on designing airplanes for the Luftwaffe. In his spare time, he created the electromechanical Zuse Z2. After about a year he left the armed forces and continued his development work on his next machine, the Z3.

The Zuse Z3, completed in 1941, was the first fully functional, program-controlled, general purpose digital computer in the world. It performed about three, or four additions per second, and multiplied in from four to five seconds. The program was entered by means of a movie film with punched holes to represent instructions. The Z3 was used in the German aircraft industry.

Later on in World War II, Zuse founded his own small business, the Zuse Apparatebau. The firm built special computers for use in the

> Of one thing I am sure—computer development has still a long way to go. Young people have got plenty of work ahead of them yet!
>
> Konrad Zuse

The Zuse Z3, completed in 1941, was the first fully functional, program-controlled, general-purpose digital comptuer. It has floating point and built-in decimal/binary conversion. The Z3 performed about three or four additions per second, and multiplied in from four to five seconds. The program was entered by means of a movie film, eight-hole channels being punched in the reel to represent instructions. Commands available were Add, Subtract, Divide, Extract Square Root, Mulltiply by 2, Multiply by 10, Multiply by 01, Multiply by .5, and Multiply by -1. Control circuits were composed of step-switches and chains of relays. There were 2600 relays in the computer. Data were entered through a keyboard providing for four decimal numbers positioned with decimal point. Output likewise consisted of four decimal digits, displayed by light bulbs on the console.

production of guided missiles. These computers, a forbearer of modern process control computers, were in operation day and night from 1942 to 1944. During this period, Zuse built the Zuse Z4, an improved version of the Zuse Z3, but still with electromagnetic arithmetic unit and mechanical memory. This machine was the only survivor of World War II. Following the war, Zuse reconditioned the Z4, equipped it with punched tape input for data and with conditional transfer instructions, and installed it at the Eidgenossische Technische Hochschule in Zurich. Five years later, the Zuse Z4 was sold to the French Department of Defense, where it was used for another four years. The computer was so reliable that it was customary to let it work through the night unattended.

In 1945, Zuse developed a universal formula language that he called *Plankalkul*. This language was the forerunner of modern programming languages. Zuse believed that the prototype language could be used for more than mathematical problems. A year later, he tried to interest IBM in his work. But neither IBM nor anyone else expressed any interest until 1949, when Remington Rand Switzerland offered him support. By that time, however, Zuse had set up his own computer manufacturing company, Zuse KG.

Zuse went on to develop other computers: the Zuse Z5, a relay machine that was six times faster than the Z4; the Zuse Z11, a relay machine; the Zuse Z22, an electronic computer with electron tubes; and the Zuse Z23, a transistorized computer. In 1958, Zuse designed a computer-controlled plotter called Zuse Z64 or Graphomat. After a number of financial difficulties, Zuse left his company, which was absorbed by Siemens AG, a large German electronic company, in 1969.

Konrad Zuse received several honorary doctorate degrees, awards and medals. He died in Hunfeld, Germany on December 18, 1995.

GEORGE STIBITZ

1904-1995

George Robert Stibitz was born on April 30, 1904 in York, Pennsylvania. He grew up in Dayton, Ohio attending an experimental and advanced high school established by Charles Kettering and some associates from Delco. The school was quite informal and the science program heavily oriented toward individual projects. When Stibitz went to college he concentrated on experimental physics and mathematics. He received a Masters degree from Union College in 1927, and spent the following year making radio propagation measurements for the General Electric Company. This work was performed in an isolated farmhouse, and he and his partner rigged a voice-actuated electrical communication link that allowed them to operate their equipment from remote control.

After the year with General Electric, Stibitz went to Cornell University for his Ph.D. in mathematical physics. In 1930 he joined Bell Laboratories as a research mathematician and became involved with investigations into circuit theory. This work eventually led him into relay circuit problems.

One evening in 1937, Stibitz brought home a couple of relays, some flashlight batteries and bulbs, and wired up a simple binary adder. This was a significant event because although he had been introduced to the notion of binary arithmetic in his high school math book, this was one of the first times that anyone had successfully adapted the concept to mechanical computation.

Stibitz soon realized he was on to something. He took his tiny binary adding circuit into his colleagues at Bell Laboratories and pointed out that this was the basis of a machine which could cope with any number of binary digits, and thus, could solve computational problems. He later designed a circuit for an electromechanical calculator that could multiply and divide complex numbers. Stibitz's Complex Number Calculator was completed in 1939. It could add and subtract three times faster than had before been possible. It was a reliable machine that used a checking feature to prevent it from producing incorrect answers.

Another notable feature of this machine was that it could be operated from a remote teletypewriter terminal. At Bell Laboratories several remote terminals, on various floors, were connected by wires to the Complex Number Calculator. This remote feature was common to Bell Lab engineers. In 1940, Stibitz first introduced remote data processing to a group of mathematicians at Dartmouth College. By renting a telephone line back to his machine at Bell Laboratories he was able to demonstrate the device working remotely.

Over the next few years, Stibitz made several proposals to Bell Laboratories to extend the design of the relay computer into new areas—requests that the company rejected. After building four more models of his Complex Number Calculator for Bell Laboratories, Stibitz left the company to be an independent consultant in snowy Vermont. In 1966, he joined the Dartmouth Medical School to apply computers and mathematics to complex biomedical problems. Stibitz continued to do research at Dartmouth until his death in 1995.

The calculating unit of complex Number Calculator, Model I. The Model I was the first relay computer in the United States to employ binary components and to use the excess-three code.

The Complex Number Calculator, Model V. This model was a system of six arithmetic units and 10 problem solving positions, an arrangement permitting the arithmetic units to function continuously. Built from parts found in ordinary telephone systems, they required only simple maintenance. Consequently, their reliability was outstanding—the Model V worked an average of twenty-two hours a day.

HOWARD AIKEN

1900-1973

Howard Hathaway Aiken was born March 8, 1900, in Hoboken, New Jersey. He grew up in Indianapolis, Indiana, where he attended high school while working 12 hours a night at a utility company. He later obtained his B.A. degree in electrical engineering in 1923 at the University of Wisconsin and his Ph.D. in 1939 at Harvard University.

In 1936, after reading Charles Babbage's original works thoughtfully, Aiken began to wonder whether it might be possible to combine into one unit a collection of the more effective calculating machines of the time. After some study he decided that a lash-up of

73

special-purpose machines would be a waste of time, and that the only way to achieve a general purpose calculator would be to start from the ground up.

Aiken served as general editor and coauthor of *The Annals of the Computation Laboratory of Harvard University*, which was composed of more than twenty-four volumes of mathematical tables, books on switching circuits and proceedings of international symposia on the theory of switching.

Beginning in 1939, Howard Aiken of Harvard, in association with IBM Corporation engineers, worked for five years to construct a fully automatic calculator using standard business-machine components. This machine was called the Automatic Sequence Controlled Calculator (also called the Harvard Mark I), and was completed in February 1944. The ASCC was something of a halfway house between the mechanical design of Babbage and the electronic designs which followed. It was an electromechanical machine approximately 51 feet (15.3 meters) long and 8 feet (2.4 meters) high. All numbers were represented to 23 decimal digits. It could perform five fundamental operations: addition, subtraction, multiplication, division, and table reference. Instructions were fed into ASCC, by punched paper tape, and the machine input was handled by punched cards. Output was either by punched cards or by printer. ASCC was a reliable and effective machine, and was used at Harvard for fifteen years, calculating astronomical tables. ASCC had more than 750,000 parts and used over 500 miles (800 kilometers) of wire.

The Automatic Sequence Controlled Calculator, or Mark I was used by the U.S. Navy for work in gunnery, ballistics, and design. Continuing his work, Aiken completed an improved Mark II in 1947, and in 1950, an all-electronic machine, the Mark III. The Mark IV was an all-electronic machine built for the U.S. Air Force in 1952. With the completion of Mark IV, Aiken got out of the business of building computers.

Author William Rodgers tells a fascinating story about Aiken in *Think*, an authoritative biography on IBM.

While the scientist was serving as a Lieutenant Commander in the Navy during World War II, Aiken and a team were sent to inspect an unexploded German torpedo. Because of its new and innovative circuitry, the torpedo was considered to be a great find, but it had to be disarmed. Much to the consternation of the other members of the Navy team, Aiken disarmed the torpedo himself. Later, when he was asked why he had taken such a risk, Aiken remarked: "Lieutenant Commanders were a dime a dozen." Aiken's remark led an old friend at Harvard to say: "What Howard just didn't realize was that Howard Aikens weren't a dime a dozen either."

During his twenty-two year tenure at Harvard University, Aiken served as a director of its fledgling Computation Laboratory, which probed such fields as automatic language translation, switching theory, and mathematical linguistics. He left Harvard in 1961 for the University of Miami, where he became a distinguished professor of information technology. Aiken also helped the University develop a computer science program and design a computing center. At a testimonial dinner that same year, Aiken voiced his concerns about his creation: "I hope to God this will be used for the benefit of mankind and not for its detriment."

He held honorary degrees from many universities. He received the Ralph E. Hackett Award in 1954, the U.S. Navy Distinguished Public Service Award in 1955, the U.S. Air Force Exceptional Civilian Service Award in 1957, and the John Price Wetherill Medal from the Franklin Institute in 1964. He was named an IEEE Fellow in 1960 for his contributions to the development of computer science and technology.

Aiken was a man of rare vision, whose insights have had a profound effect on the entire computing profession. He shared many of his ideas to scholarly journals in computer technology, switching theory and electronics.

In 1944, Harvard University's Howard Aiken and IBM completed five years of work on the Automatic Sequence Controlled Calculator (ASCC) or Harvard Mark I, the largest electromechanical calculator ever built. It had 3300 relays and weighed 5 tons. It could multiply two 23-digit numbers in six seconds.

Howard Aiken examining a paper tape control reader in the Automatic Sequence Controlled Calculator.

Aiken was in his 73rd year when he died in his sleep in St. Louis, Missouri on March 14, 1973. He had made his home in Fort Lauderdale, Florida, where he lived with his wife Mary.

The Harvard Mark IV calculator.

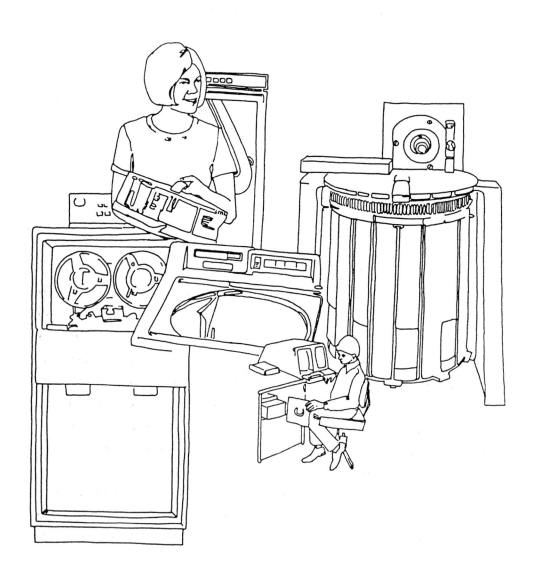

THE BEGINNING
OF ELECTRONIC
COMPUTERS

World War II made the computer more vital than ever as the need for ever faster computations kept mounting. Among other problems was the calculation of great quantities of ballistic tables for newly designed artillery weapons. Military specialists required nearly seven hours at desk calculators to compute a single trajectory. Although the early relay computers were ten times faster than desk calculators and could work for days without human intervention, they were slow by present-day standards because the relay contacts took too long to open and close. Fortunately, a faster electric switch, the vacuum tube was at hand.

In 1942 John Vincent Atanasoff of Iowa State College and Clifford Berry, his graduate student, completed work on an electronic vacuum tube computer. The ABC (Atanasoff-Berry Computer) is recognized today as the first true electronic digital computer. Atanasoff is credited by many historians as being the father of the electronic computer.

While Atanasoff was working on the ABC, he met and discussed his project with John W. Mauchly of the University of Pennsylvania. From their discussions Mauchly devised his own ideas on how to build a better computer. He teamed up with J. Presper Eckert, and together they built the first large-scale general-purpose electronic digital computer, the ENIAC (Electronic Numerical Integrator And Computer). The ENIAC was funded by the U.S. Army as the need for computing accurate ballistic tables increased during World War II. The ENIAC was a far more important machine than the ABC and was used for many years to perform substantial computing work.

Even before ENIAC was completed, plans were being drawn for an even more sophisticated computer, the EDVAC (Electronic Discrete Variable Automatic Computer). A Hungarian-born, naturalized American logician, John von Neumann proposed that the computer's memory areas contain programming instructions as well as data. This stored program concept is used in all modern computers. Many historians consider this stored program concept among the most important developments in the computer field in the twentieth century.

While the EDVAC was being developed, a team headed by Maurice Wilkes at the University of Cambridge in England developed the EDSAC (Electronic Delay Storage Automatic Calculator). EDSAC also incorporated the stored program concept.

Mauchly and Eckert, who developed the ENIAC, later designed and built the first commercial computer, Univac I (Universal Automatic Computer). Over the years, there have been many significant advancements in the developing technology of computers.

Although most computers were still too expensive to be purchased by a small business, yet the trend and philosophy of industry was headed in a direction that demanded attention. Norbert Wiener of the Massachusetts Institute of Technology had pointed out in 1948, in his book *Cybernetics*, that the age of brute force had reached a peak. From now on, emphasis must be on control of power, on communications, and on automatic processes. Robots, Wiener pointed out, would inevitably take over many tasks performed by humans.

Several years before the beginning of modern computer technology, British mathematician Alan M. Turing proposed a computing concept now known as the *Turing machine*. This machine has never been built, however, it is useful for checking out possible approaches to problem solving and as a tool for teaching students the fundamentals of computing.

JOHN ATANASOFF

1903-1995

John Vincent Atanasoff was born on October 4, 1903 in Hamilton, New York. His Bulgarian father graduated from Colgate University and his mother was a high school graduate but knew mathematics perfectly. When he was nine years old, his father, an electrical engineer, gave him a slide rule and set of instructions. Atanasoff mastered most simple problems in trigonometry, calculus, radio theory and physics, and found his life transformed by this newly discovered problem solving ability. Early in high school he decided to make theoretical physics not just a career, but his life's work.

He received his B.S. at Florida State in 1925, his M.S. at Iowa State in 1926, and his Ph.D. at the University of Wisconsin in 1930. After receiving his doctorate, he returned to Iowa State College (now Iowa State University) where he remained until 1945 as a professor in mathematics and physics. In the late 1930s he began thinking about ways to simplify the myriad computations necessary for his research. Breakthroughs in electronics, such as the invention of the vacuum tube and condenser in the 20th century, offered professionals like Atanasoff the opportunity to discover new ways to compute faster and more accurately. He got hung up on a basic problem: How do you get the machine to remember what it has already done? A long, aimless drive from Iowa to Illinois ended in a bar and led to an inspiration. Through electronics, he used a base two binary format—which uses the digits 1 and 0 as its basis. In 1939 Atanasoff, along with graduate student Clifford Berry, devised a machine that satisfied the four basic precepts of computing. It had input and output. It held data that could be modified. It had a memory. And it worked!

As completed in 1942, the Atanasoff-Berry Computer (ABC) consisted of two 1500-bit drums for storing 50-bit words, 300 vacuum tubes, a spark printer and reader, and an electronic adder circuit. Atanasoff's machine was unique and inventive in the following respects: Memory held data by continually regenerating its contents, calculations were performed in serial fashion, calculating logic was represented by circuitry, and it operated digitally. A historic decision by the U.S. District Court in 1973 declared the ABC to be the first computing device that was all electronic in design and utilized the binary numbering system, regenerative memory, and digital arithmetic circuitry. These characteristics are still found in modern-day computers. Up until 1973, credit for the first electronic computer was traditionally given to John W. Mauchly and J. Presper Eckert for the ENIAC.

In 1939, John Atanasoff built the prototype of an electronic digital computer. With the help of an assistant, Clifford Berry, the ABC (Atanasoff-Berry Computer) was assembled in 1942. The ABC was the first electronic digital computer. It used vacuum tubes as the logic elements within the machine.

Besides his inventing work, Atanasoff was a businessman whose firm, Ordnance Engineering Corp., was sold to Aerojet General in 1962. He holds approximately thirty patents.

The awards Atanasoff has received for his work in computing include the Order of Cyril and Methodius, First Class, Bulgaria's highest honor for scientists, in 1970, and two honorary doctor of science degrees. Atanasoff has also devoted more than a decade to another project—developing a new universal alphabet. Unfortunately, the rest of the world has not shown much enthusiasm toward the project.

Atanasoff died of a stroke on June 15, 1995, at his home in Monrovia, Maryland. Although the debate about his and John Mauchly's work continues in professional circles, most of the world agrees that Atanasoff is the inventor of the first electronic digital computer.

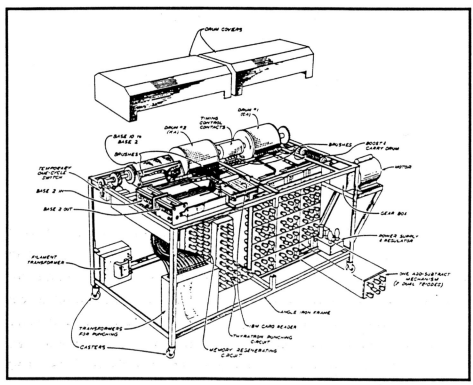

Drawing of the ABC (Atanasoff Berry Computer).

J. PRESPER ECKERT

1919-1995

J. Presper Eckert was born on April 9, 1919, the only child of prosperous Philadelphia parents. Eckert had a stimulating childhood peopled with such figures as Douglas Fairbanks, Sr., Charlie Chaplin, and President Warren Harding, and punctuated with world travel totaling 125,000 miles by the age of twelve. The Hollywood stars were colleagues in John Presper Eckert, Sr.'s World War I bond drive efforts and the travel included the elder Eckert's business and vacation trips.

In 1937, Eckert graduated from the William Penn Charter School, the oldest private boys' school in the United States. He breezed through his regular courses and took on two years of college math, as well. Eckert received a bachelor of science degree in electrical engineering from the University of Pennsylvania's Moore School of Electrical Engineering in 1941. After graduation, he stayed at the University to teach, do research, and pursue graduate studies.

It was in Eckert's role as lab instructor, at age twenty-two, that he met thirty-four-year-old John Mauchly. During an eight week government-paid defense course in electronics, Eckert and Mauchly discussed what they both wanted to do—build a computer. Two years later, Eckert received his master's degree in electrical engineering and the two joined forces to begin work on their first computer. In Mauchly, Eckert had found a mind that complemented his almost perfectly, and did so for many years. It was a team like Rodgers and Hammerstein or Gilbert and Sullivan, a perfect blend of complementary talents that time after time produced compelling works that would eventually enchant millions.

Both were already interested in the possibilities of automatic computation when World War II turned possibilities into urgent needs. In 1942, the Ballistic Research Laboratory of the U.S. Army Ordnance Department was assigned the job of recomputing firing and bombing tables for guns being used in World War II, and for proposed guns, rockets, missiles, and other strategic arms.

In 1942, Eckert and Mauchly submitted a proposal to the U.S. Army describing an electronic computer, which resulted in a contract from the Army's Ordnance Department to build the machine. Eckert, the only full-time person on the project, served as project manager. Mauchly, who was teaching full-time, found himself consultant to a team of fifty people (at its largest) assigned to build the computer. Begun in April 1943, on Eckert's twenty-fourth birthday, ENIAC was completed more than 200,000 people-hours later, 3 years after it was started. ENIAC, which stands for Electronic Numerical Integrator

ENIAC (Electronic Numerical Integrator And Computer), the first large-scale electronic digital computer, was built by J. Presper Eckert and John Mauchly at the Moore School of Electrical Engineering, University of Pennsylvania in 1946. It was used by the U.S. Army to compute trajectories for new weapons.

And Computer, was unveiled in formal dedication ceremonies on February 16, 1946. Flawlessly, it completed its first problem: a highly secret numerical simulation for the yet-untested hydrogen bomb. This exercise, which would have taken existing calculating machines 40 hours, took ENIAC twenty seconds.

The ENIAC was literally a giant. It contained 18,000 vacuum tubes, weighed 30 tons, and occupied a room the size of an average three-bedroom home. It was capable of performing 5,000 additions per second. This was considerably faster than any existing device or any machine that was even under development elsewhere. ENIAC functioned until October 2, 1955, when it was dismantled and part of it was sent to the Smithsonian Institution in Washington, D.C., where it became part of an exhibit on computing.

During the course of development work on ENIAC, Eckert and Mauchly and their associates recognized many deficiencies in this device. In 1944, the Moore School obtained a supplement to the ENIAC contract for the development of the Electronic Discrete Variable Automatic Computer (EDVAC). This computer was to be a stored-program computer with a 1,000-word capacity that would use mercury delay lines for storing data. During the next 18 months, Eckert and Mauchly and their associates completed ENIAC and began development of EDVAC. John von Neumann became a consultant to the Moore School and assisted the staff in formalizing the stored-program concept for this computer.

Eckert and Mauchly left the University of Pennsylvania in 1947 to form their own company, the Eckert-Mauchly Computer Corporation, where they developed the Binary Automatic Computer (BINAC) in 1949. BINAC was the first computer to be programmed by internally stored instructions (EDVAC would not be completed until 1952).

BINAC was never more to Eckert and Mauchly than a steppingstone to their next computer—Univac I. The two men believed in the commercial potential of computers. By the fall of 1949, the Eckert-Mauchly firm was in financial difficulties. A year later the company was sold to Remington Rand. In 1951, Univac I was delivered to the Bureau of the Census. Univac I was America's first general-purpose commercial computer able to handle a wide variety of applications.

Both Eckert and Mauchly had become employees of the Remington Rand Corporation (which later became Sperry Rand Corporation and then Unisys Corporation). After almost two decades of working together, the Eckert-Mauchly team split up in 1959 and Eckert went on to become the director of the Univac Division. In 1955, he was named vice-president and director of research at Univac. Eight years later, Eckert was appointed vice-president and technical advisor for computer systems at Sperry. Eckert received an honorary degree of doctor of science in engineering from the University

The Univac I computer was used to predict the outcome of the 1952 presidential election. Walter Cronkite (right), veteran CBS anchorman, is being shown the machine by J. Presper Eckert (center). In the early hours CBS did not trust its projection of an Eisenhower sweep.

of Pennsylvania in 1964. Between 1948 and 1966 Eckert received eighty-five patents, mostly for electronic inventions. In 1969, Eckert was awarded the National Science Foundation's National Medal of Science, the nation's highest award for distinguished achievement in science, mathematics, and engineering. Eckert died in 1995.

Shown here is a close-up view of some of the ENIAC panels, the digit busses, program busses, control switches and indicator lamps. J. Presper Eckert is changing a switch setting. Stories are told about how all the lights in West Philadelphia would dim when ENIAC was turned on, and how the starting transient would always burn out at least three or more tubes.

JOHN MAUCHLY

1907-1980

John William Mauchly was born in Cincinnati, Ohio, on August 30, 1907. His father was a physicist at the Department of Terrestrial Magnetism of the Carnegie Institution in Washington, D.C. Mauchly grew up in Chevy Chase, Maryland. He attended John Hopkins University on a scholarship, receiving a doctoral degree in physics in 1932 at the age of 24.

The following year he became a professor of physics at Ursinus College in Collegeville, Pennsylvania, near Philadelphia. During his eight years at Ursinus, he began a project on weather analysis that led him to the conviction that a high-speed computer was necessary. Realizing that the speed problem could be solved by electronics, he began experimenting with equipment he purchased himself.

In 1941, Mauchly left Ursinus College to join the staff of the Moore School of Electrical Engineering at the University of Pennsylvania, in Philadelphia. It was there that he met J. Presper Eckert.

The following year, Mauchly and Eckert submitted a proposal to the U.S. Army describing an electronic computer, which resulted in a contract from the Army's Ordnance Department to build the machine.

Basically conceived to help develop new weapons during World War II, the Electronics Numerical Integrator And Computer (ENIAC) was completed in 1946. It was this nation's first large-scale electronic digital computer and it was certainly a landmark leading to the development of many future computer designs.

Mauchly was an idea man of tremendously good instincts. He was a conceptualizer, a catalyst, and a pioneer who championed ideas before their time. He was certainly the prime mover in securing the contract for the first large-scale electronic digital computer. He was one of the founders and early president of the Association for Computing Machinery (ACM) and the Society for Industrial and Applied Mathematics (SIAM).

Both Mauchly and Eckert had become employees of the Remington Rand Corporation, which later became Sperry Rand Corporation and then Unisys Corporation.

In 1959, Mauchly left Sperry Rand and his partner of eighteen years to form Mauchly Associates. While working in his own company, Mauchly developed the critical path method (CPM) for job and resource scheduling. In 1968, Mauchly formed Dynatrend, a systems consulting company that specialized in forecasting weather and stock market trends.

Mauchly died January 8, 1980, while undergoing heart surgery in Ambler, Pennsylvania. He was 72 years old.

The co-inventors of the ENIAC, J. Presper Eckert (left) and John Mauchly (right), are shown with the machine. The equipment weighed more than 30 tons and occupied more than 1,500 square feet. It had some 18,000 vacuum tubes and was able to perform 5,000 calculations per second.

This Philadelphia Evening Bulletin newspaper cartoon suggests that ENIAC might be able to solve the perplexing wage-price problems that faced these three politicians in 1946.

The first Univac I computer was installed at the Bureau of the Census in 1951. The inventors of ENIAC and Univac I, Mauchly and Eckert, are shown standing by the console on the left.

ALAN TURING

1912-1954

Alan Mathison Turing was born at Warrington Crescent in London, England, on June 23, 1912, of upper-middle-class, well-educated parents. Turing showed his brilliance early. Around his third birthday, his mother wrote to his father, who was frequently away from home on business, that Alan was "a very clever child, I should say, with a wonderful memory for new words. Alan generally speaks correctly and well. He has rather a delightful phrase, 'for so many morrows,' which we think means 'for a long time,' and is used with reference to past or future."

When Turing was six years old, he found a copy of *Reading Without Tears*, and taught himself the rudiments of reading in about three weeks. At the age of nine he is said to have startled his mother, out of the blue, with the question, "Mother, what makes the oxygen fit so tightly into the hydrogen to produce water?"

In preparatory school, Turing looked on sports as a waste of time, although years later he would become a first-class marathon runner. His mathematics teacher claimed that Turing was "a mathematician, I think." Not yet fifteen years of age, he had already evolved the calculus term "$\tan^{-1} x$," without any knowledge of calculus.

From his early days at school, Turing cared only about mathematics and science. He was conscious of his own scientific genius at an early age, and was sufficiently aware of it to write to his mother from school: "I always seem to want to make things from the thing that is commonest in nature and with the least waste of energy." He left the Sherborne School loaded with mathematics prizes and a scholarship to King's College, Cambridge.

He went to King's College in 1931. In 1935 he began work in mathematical logic and started on his best-known investigation on computable numbers. In 1937, Turing published his famous paper, *On Computable Numbers with an Application to the Entscheidungsproblem*. In that paper, he envisioned the Turing machine, which could be fed instructions from punched paper tape. Two years after being graduated from King's College, Turing was invited to Princeton University, where he earned his doctorate in 1938. Turing contemplated staying in the United States and was offered a post as assistant to John von Neumann, but in 1938 he decided to return to Cambridge. Shortly after he returned to Cambridge, the war broke out and he spent the next six years with the Foreign Office.

During World War II, Turing was one of a team of British scientists sequestered at the Bletchley Park estate and ordered to develop machinery that could decipher codes from Germany's Enigma encoding machines. The results of these efforts, often credited with a decisive role in winning the war, were several electromechanical machines. The successor to these machines, the Colossus code-breaking computer, is now accepted as the first operational electronic computer.

In 1945, he joined the staff of the National Physical Laboratory to work on the design, construction, and use of a large automatic computer that he named the Automatic Computing Engine (ACE). About 1949 he became deputy director of the Computing Laboratory at the University of Manchester where the Manchester Automatic Digital Machine (MADM), the computer with the largest memory capacity in the world at that time, was being built. His efforts in the construction of early computers and the development of early programming techniques were of prime importance.

Turing spent a major part of his life trying to answer the question, Can a machine think? His interest in this problem was stimulated by talks with Norbert Wiener, the founder of cybernetics, whom Turing first met on visits to America. Wiener, applying the mechanism of computers to human behavior, believed that mental disorders are primarily diseases of the memory. The question of thinking machines and their possibilities is frightening. If machines think, then is human thinking just a mechanical activity? If so, then where does one's potential lie? As greater machines develop where will their capacities end?

Turing believed that machines do think and explained his position in an article, "Can a Machine Think?" As a practical demonstration he designed a machine that simulated human thinking by playing off a single move in a chess game. He succeeded in proving that machines can perform deductive analysis by solving mathematical equations and making logical decisions.

At the peak of his career and in the prime of life, Alan Turing was found dead in bed, on June 8, 1954, at the age of 42. His death was caused by poisoning from potassium cyanide, ruled at the inquest to have been self-administered.

The Association for Computing Machinery (ACM) has annually given its highest award, the Turing Award, for technical contributions to the computing community. Alan Turing's name and influence live on. His work remains relevant even in today's world of advanced research.

COMPUTER

EXAMINER   HUMAN PLAYER

Turing's test developed by British mathematician Alan Turing, is a game to determine whether a computer might be considered to possess intelligence. Participants in the game include two respondents (a comptuer and a human) and a human examiner who tries to determine which of the unseen respondents is the human. According to this test, intelligence and the ability to think would be demonstrated by the comptuer's success in fooling the examiner.

JOHN von NEUMANN

1903-1957

John von Neumann was born in Budapest, Hungary, on December 28, 1903. A child prodigy, he could read Latin and Greek at age five. As a six-year-old he could divide two eight-digit numbers in his head. At eight years of age, he had mastered that difficult branch of mathematics known as calculus.

Von Neumann came out of an upper-class Hungarian background that produced other giants in mathematics and physics. His father, a Jewish banker named Max Neumann, earned sufficient respect to add the honorific "Margattai" to his family name (later changed, by John, to "von"). John was the eldest of three sons.

Even as a child, John loved mathematics and constantly sought to adapt its logic to the world at large. From 1911 to 1916, he attended the Lutheran gymnasium in Budapest, becoming its best mathematician. Though he enrolled in the University of Budapest in 1921, von Neumann acquired the bulk of his education at other institutions. Most of his time, especially from 1921 to 1923, was spent at the University of Berlin. There he listened to lectures by Albert Einstein. Von Neumann went on to the Swiss Federal Institute of Technology in Zurich, where he received a diploma in chemical engineering in 1925. In 1926, he received a doctoral degree in mathematics from the University of Budapest. Studying at the University of Göttingen in 1926 and 1927, von Neumann mixed with some of the most superb minds in mathematics.

Between 1927 and 1930 von Neumann was a lecturer in mathematics at the University of Berlin. Rarely had one so young held that post. During his first year there, he published five papers. Three of them, by setting out a mathematical framework for quantum theory, were of great importance to that field. A fourth paper was a pioneering effort in game theory. The fifth dealt with the link between formal logic systems and the limits of mathematics. By the 1930s, von Neumann was recognized as one of the world's leading mathematicians.

In 1930, Princeton University invited him to be a visiting lecturer, an appointment he held for three years. In 1933, he received a permanent position at Princeton's newly created Institute for Advanced Study.

With the onset of World War II, von Neumann's knowledge of mathematical physics proved of great value to his adopted country. His contributions to supersonic wind tunnel development and solutions to nonlinear systems of equations and implosion were instrumental in advancing the Allied cause.

During and after the war, his main professional interest shifted from pure to applied mathematics.

Von Neumann did important work in many branches of advanced mathematics. For one thing, he made a thorough study of quantum mechanics and showed that Schrödinger's wave mechanics and Heisenberg's matrix mechanics were mathematically equivalent.

Even more important was his development of a new branch of mathematics called "game theory". He had written on the subject as early as 1928, but his complete book, *The Theory of Games and Economic Behavior*, did not appear until 1944. This branch of mathematics is called game theory because it works out the best strategies to follow in simple games, such as coin matching; however, the principles will apply to far more complicated games such as business and war, where an attempt is made to work out the best strategy to beat a competitor or an enemy.

Von Neumann early recognized the importance of computing devices. A major advance in computer design occurred in 1946 when he reintroduced the stored-program idea and revolutionized the technology of computing. Von Neumann suggested that programs (instructions for problem solutions) be stored in the computer's memory until needed. Prior to this time programs were contained on wired control panels or punched cards, both external to the computer. With the programs in the computer, instructions could be manipulated and modified by machine commands.

In 1947, von Neumann suggested a method for converting ENIAC, an early electronic computer, into a stored-program machine. His extraordinary skill in mathematical operations contributed to the development of the computer known as MANIAC (Mathematical Analyzer, Numerical Integrator And Computer). This computer enabled the United States to produce and test (first test, 1952) the world's first hydrogen bomb.

Von Neumann was a generalist among contemporary scientists. His clarity and precision of thought had a profound impact in many areas from which we will continue to benefit in the years ahead. He was one of the most respected scientists of his time. Von Neumann died in 1957 at the early age of fifty-four from cancer.

John von Neumann and the IAS (Institute for Advanced Study) Computer. This computer occupied 100 square feet of floor space and contained 2,300 vacuum tubes. The cylinders protruding from the lower section of the computer are part of the cathode ray tube memory.

MAURICE WILKES

born 1913

Maurice Vincent Wilkes did his undergraduate and graduate studies at Cambridge University in England. In 1937, he received a Ph.D. degree for a thesis on the propagation of very long radio waves in the ionosphere. Wilkes became director of the Mathematics Laboratory at Cambridge after World War II. He headed the team that developed EDSAC (Electronic Delayed Storage Automatic Computer), which stored 512 words of 34 bits each. The EDSAC, which boasted 3,000 electronic values, could add two numbers in 70 microseconds, multiplying them in 8.5 milliseconds. But where the mighty machine really scored was in its storage—both programs and data could be contained in the same store, which allowed greater flexibility in programming. EDSAC ran its first stored program in May 1949.

Working with engineers from the London bakery firm of J. Lyons & Co., the Wilkes team helped to build another computer, the Lyons Electronic Office (LEO) in 1951. Similar in design to EDSAC, LEO was designed to be used purely for commercial data handling.

Wilkes was elected a Fellow of the Royal Society in 1956 and in 1957, he became the first president of the British Computer Society. He later worked for Digital Equipment Corporation (DEC) in Great Britain. In 1980 he became a Senior Consulting Engineer with DEC in Maynard, Massachusetts. On returning to England, he became a member of the research board of Italian computer manufacturer, Olivetti.

A general view of EDSAC.

NORBERT WIENER

1894-1964

Norbert Wiener was born on November 26, 1984 in Columbia, Missouri, the oldest child of Leo Wiener, an immigrant Russian Jew and professor of Slavic languages at Harvard University. Young Wiener was clearly a prodigy. He began reading when he was three, he graduated in 1909 from Tufts College with a degree in mathematics at the age of fourteen, and earned his doctorate at Harvard University in 1913, before his nineteenth birthday. In 1919 he joined the faculty of the Massachusetts Institute of Technology. Wiener remained on the MIT faculty, eventually becoming one of its most famous members, until his retirement.

In 1926, he married Margaret Engemans and together they had two daughters. Both he and his family travelled extensively during the period 1926-30; to Europe on several occasions, where Wiener worked with leading mathematicians of his time; and to China for a year in 1935.

During World War II Wiener worked on gunfire control, the problem of pointing a gun to fire at a moving target. The ideas that evolved led Wiener to co-discover the theory concerning the prediction of stationary time series. It introduced certain statistical methods into control and communications engineering and exerted great influence in these areas. This work also led him to formulate the concept of cybernetics.

In 1948 his book *Cybernetics* appeared. For a scientific book it was extremely popular, and Wiener became known in a much broader scientific community than just that of mathematics. Cybernetics is the theoretical study of control processes in electronics and mechanical and biological systems, especially the mathematical analysis of the flow of information in such systems. It is used today in control theory, automation theory, and computer programs to reduce many time-consuming computations and decision making processes formerly done by human beings. Wiener worked at cybernetics, philosophized for it the rest of his life, all the while keeping up his research in other area of mathematics.

After World War II he announced he would contribute no further to any form of military research, and spent the rest of his life trying to alert humanity to the significance and problems of the coming age of automation.

Wiener was reportedly extremely absent minded. One story tells of how he was stopped by a friend one day while walking on the MIT campus. He terminated the conversation, then asked, "When you stopped me, which way was I going?" Given the answer, he replied, "Ah, Then I've had lunch."

Norbert Wiener, the father of cybernetics, helped explain the meaning of computers. He was active in professional societies in the United States and abroad. He also received many honors such as the National Medal of Science for achievement in both mathematics and biological sciences. He was one of the outstanding mathematicians and scientists of the United States. He died on March 19, 1964 in Stockholm, Sweden.

> *This piece of work is an example of the value and even necessity of combining the machine and the living organism, of combining control and communication too, into a unified subject. I've called it **cybernetics**.*
>
> Norbert Wiener

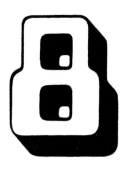

MODERN
COMPUTERS

The ABC, ENIAC, EDVAC, EDSAC, and Univac I were some of the first electronic computers, and they used vacuum tubes as the basic counting device. During the 1950s many of these vacuum tube computers were built and marketed. The computation speed was in the range of 1000 to 5000 additions per second, a tremendous increase in computational speed over pre-computer days.

In 1947 an electronic device called a transistor was invented by physicists at Bell Laboratories. This device could perform most of the functions that a vacuum tube could perform but much faster, consumed only a fraction of the energy required by vacuum tubes, and created only a small amount of heat. It seemed to be the answer for computer designers of the late 1950s and very early 1960s who had been fighting the problem of keeping computer rooms cool enough that these electronic marvels would operate properly. Thus, from 1958 to 1964 a large number of transistor computers were built and marketed. These computers had calculating speeds ranging from 2,000 additions per second for the small machines to 500,000 per second for large machines.

In 1957 the first integrated circuit was produced and after 1964, it would have a tremendous effect on computer development. An integrated circuit (IC) is a device that combines all of the capabilities of many transistors and other circuit components into one tiny "chip" of solid material about one-sixteenth of an inch square and a few hundredths of an inch thick. This marvelous electronic device is manufactured by a mechanized microphotographic process, hence the cost of production is very low. Therefore, not only does the IC make it possible to construct still faster computers with larger memories than ever, but the cost of a given computer is less than it was before. Computers using integrated circuits perform as many as 10 million additions per second.

In 1965 the Digital Equipment Corporation introduced the first minicomputer. Minicomputers were smaller and less expensive than the large computers. Even small businesses could afford them. In the early 1970s computers started using LSI Llarge Scale Integration) circuit chips. The number of transistors that can be placed on one chip is truly incredible. For example, a computer using LSI chips with 100,000 or more transistors can do the same work as the earlier room-size computers. Sometime later, computers were using VLSI (Very Large Scale Integration) chips which contained as many as 500,000 transistors.

With so many circuits now located on a chip, it was only a matter of time before someone got the idea that one chip could contain all the circuits necessary to perform the basic functions of an entire computer. In 1969 the microprocessor was developed. The microprocessor was a general-purpose computer that could be programmed to do any number of tasks, from producing a business report to guiding a space vehicle. Companies in a variety of fields rushed to take advantage of the microprocessor's power. The microprocessor inevitably made possible the microcomputer, a compact relatively inexpensive, complete computer. Several microcomputers were made available in the mid-1970s. Stephen Wozniak and Steven Jobs made the microcomputer even more accessible by combining its components on a single circuit board. This Apple I computer was revised into Apple II, and Apple Computer, Inc. was born.

Many people were associated with the transition of computers from the vacuum tube computers of the 1950s to the microcomputers of today. The people discussed in this book are Thomas J. Watson, Sr., who made the IBM Corporation a powerhouse in the computer industry; William C. Norris, who produced Control Data Corporation computers; Seymour Cray, the developer of supercomputers; Steven P. Jobs and Stephen G. Wozniak, the founders of Apple Computer, Inc. and the people largely responsible for the microcomputer revolution of today.

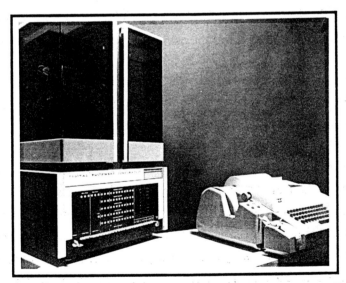

The PDP-8 minicomputer was introduced by Digital Equipment Corporation in 1965. This table-top minicomputer found widespread use in laboratories, and educational institutions.

THOMAS WATSON, SR.

1874-1956

Thomas John Watson was born on February 17, 1874, in a farmhouse in East Campbell, New York, a rural area southwest of the Finger Lakes. Watson's childhood was largely uneventful. Neither studious nor athletic, he reportedly was lively and assertive, with a quick temper that was to plague him all his life. He grew up in an ordinary but happy home where the means and wants were modest and the moral environment strict. The important values, as he learned them, were to do every job well, to treat all people with dignity and respect, to appear neatly dressed, to be clean, to be optimistic, and above all, to be loyal.

His father, a tough lumberjack with little formal education himself, held high ambitions for his son and advised him to become a lawyer. Young Watson, however, was more interested in accounting and business. After a year at the Miller School of Commerce in Elmira, New York, studying accounting and business, Watson landed a job as a bookkeeper in a meat market. He was eighteen years old and his salary was $6 a week.

He gave up his bookkeeping job to sell pianos, organs, sewing machines, and caskets with a friend, George Cornwell. Learning from Cornwell's easy manner, he developed skill in selling. This ability to observe others, focus on the good traits, and weave this into his own approach to people was to play a major role in his success.

In 1895, Watson took a selling job with National Cash Register (NCR), whose powerful president, John H. Patterson, was also to be a strong influence on his life. Four years later, he was promoted to manager in Rochester, New York. By 1907, Watson was in charge of the company's second-hand business. Now the third most powerful man at NCR, Watson was thirty-three years old.

Watson met Jeannett Kittredge, daughter of a successful Ohio businessman, in the spring of 1912. A year later they were married. They had four children: Thomas, Jr., Jane, Helen, and Arthur.

While at NCR, Watson originated his famous instruction, THINK. Framed placards with that one word appeared in the company's offices. The purpose was to inspire a dispirited NCR sales force. Later, when he took the helm at IBM, he reintroduced this motto.

He left NCR in 1913 to become president of the Computing-Tabulating-Recording (C-T-R) Company, a punched card equipment manufacturer. By introducing the selling methods successful with cash registers, he transformed C-T-R into the leading manufacturer of business machines. C-T-R had been created in 1911 by combining three separate companies, including Herman Hollerith's Tabulating

Thomas Watson, Sr. standing in front of an IBM New York showroom in the 1930s (top), and delivering a morale-boosting speech at a 1918 sales convention (bottom). Watson was best known for his marketing and management skills.

Machine Company established in 1896. Watson carried on a running battle with Hollerith, who was still involved in the company, feeling that Hollerith's technical genius was not matched by business genius. For the rest of his life Watson favored salespeople over technical people. C-T-R was renamed International Business Machines (IBM) in 1924.

Watson guided the IBM Corporation, the world's largest manufacturer of computers, throughout the rest of his life. He established a research and development group with a laboratory and a small staff of inventors. From this group came improved punched card tabulating equipment and, later, a large number of computer systems. Watson always placed heavy emphasis on education, research, and engineering to ensure the growth of the company. A great deal of Watson's success was due to his understanding of customers' needs, which resulted in steady improvements in IBM's products.

Watson demanded that his sales representatives not only sell the company's products, but come up with new ideas for their use. He also believed that they should always reflect IBM's principles: respect for the individual, service to the customer, and superior performance. Such a sales force gave IBM the reputation of being different. Its people were noticed; even on a service call, IBM employees wore suit jackets to the amazement of customers.

Watson created a corporate culture, an esprit de corps that is the envy of the business world to this day. The Watson way was also admired by President Franklin D. Roosevelt, who offered two prestigious posts to the patriotic IBM founder during World War II: Secretary of Commerce and Ambassador to Great Britain.

It was largely through Watson's efforts and funding that Howard Aiken's Mark I was built. Watson ordered his engineers to develop a new machine that could outperform the Mark I. The resultant IBM machine was the Selective Sequence Electronic Calculator (SSEC).

The Selective Sequence Electronic Calculator (SSEC) was intended
to prove that IBM could build the world's fastest calculator. Thomas
Watson's answer to the coming of the computer age. Watson had it
installed in the lobby of IBM headquarters in New York, where
scientists could come in and use it for free.

When completed in 1947, it was far more powerful and flexible than anything previously built.

Following the Korean War, IBM designed the 701 computer. One-fourth the size of the SSEC, the 701 was twenty-five times as fast, performing 21,000 calculations a second. The IBM 650 computer was released in December 1954. It was a great success. Also in the same year, the IBM 704 scientific computer was introduced. Two new IBM computers followed in 1955 and 1956, the IBM 702 and the IBM 705. By now the IBM Corporation was on its way to becoming the leader in the computer industry. Watson lived long enough to see the introduction of the 700 family of computers, IBM's first production computers.

On May 8, 1956, Watson turned over the post of chief executive officer of IBM to his eldest son, Thomas Watson, Jr. On June 19, just over a month later, Watson died of a heart attack at the age of eighty-two. His two sons both held senior executive positions within IBM and both became U.S. ambassadors, Thomas John to Moscow and the younger son, Arthur Kittredge, to Paris.

Shown standing behind the operator's console of the Selective Sequence Electronic Calculator (SSEC) is Thomas Watson, Sr. (second from the right).

WILLIAM NORRIS

born 1911

William C. Norris was born on July 14, 1911, on a farm in Red Cloud, Nebraska. Obtaining an education was not simple for Norris, He had to walk or ride a pony, no matter what the weather, to a one-room schoolhouse a mile from home. While in high school, Norris developed a strong interest in physics. In 1932 he received a bachelor's degree in electrical engineering at the University of Nebraska. With few jobs available, Norris ran the family farm for the next two years. He later took a civil engineering job that involved laying out terraces and dams.

In 1934, he joined the Westinghouse Company and sold x-ray machines and other equipment. In 1941, he took a job as an electrical engineer for the U.S. Navy in Washington, D.C. After Pearl Harbor, Norris was commissioned in the Naval Reserve, where he worked with mathematicians and engineers from corporations and universities in top-secret cryptography work, trying to break German and Japanese codes.

After the war (1946), at the government's suggestion, Norris and other technical specialists found private financing and formed Engineering Research Associates (ERA), which specialized in producing customized data processing equipment for the Navy. By 1952, ERA had built over eighty percent of all American-built electronic computers.

Engineering Research Associates was purchased by Remington Rand in 1952. After Remington Rand and Sperry Corporation merged in 1955 (becoming Sperry Rand), Norris became vice-president and general manager of the new St. Paul, Minnesota-based electronic computer division called Univac. Frustrated because Univac was not able to keep up with IBM in building and marketing new computers, Norris decided to venture out on his own. In 1957, Norris along with Seymour Cray and seven others left Sperry Rand Corporation to found Control Data Corporation (CDC). Cray was given a free rein by Norris to develop a supercomputer line. The first computer produced by CDC was the CDC 1604. When it reached the market in 1958, it was one of the first fully transistorized computers and the largest scientific computer at the time. The CDC 1604's early success was phenomenal. Control Data could not make them fast enough to keep up with the demand.

In 1959 CDC released the Model 160 desk-sized computer. A year later, Cray began working on the CDC 6600. When the CDC 6600 appeared in 1963, it was twenty times faster than any other computer. It could execute an average of over 3 million instructions per second.

Control Data Corporation continued building fast scientific computers; the next step was the CDC 7600, followed by the Star 100 in 1974. Then came the CYBER 205, one of the first supercomputers to introduce vector processing, in which the computer works on many different parts of the problem at once. The CYBER 205 is capable of up to 800 million operations a second.

By the mid-1960s, Norris had become convinced that total dependence on mainframe computers was unwise. He looked for other businesses. Norris took the company into the peripheral products business. It proved to be a wise decision. Between 1969 and 1971, when the large computer market suffered a setback, CDC was able to fall back on the peripherals business.

Norris continued to build his empire by developing a strong line of peripherals, two service bureaus, and a technology information service. The company also made substantial investments in the development of the PLATO system—computer-aided educational hardware and software.

In 1986, Norris, at age 76, retired from the company he founded twenty-nine years earlier. During his more than forty years in the computer business, he took on many very big and controversial projects.

CDC 1604 computer. In 1958, one of the first fully transistorized computers and the largest scientific computer at the time. Norris gave Seymour Cray a free rein to design the CDC 1604. It was the first comptuer developed by Control Data Corporation.

In 1963, Control Data Corporation introduced the CDC 6600 which could execute an average of over 3 million instructions per second. It was twenty times faster than any other computer.

SEYMOUR CRAY

born 1925

Seymour Cray was born in Chippewa Falls, Wisconsin, on September 28, 1925. His father was a city engineer in Chippewa Falls. After a few years as an electrician in the army, Cray began his college education at the University of Wisconsin in Madison. He later transferred to the University of Minnesota. Cray received a bachelor's degree in electrical engineering in 1950 and a master's degree in 1951.

Cray began in the computer business working for Engineering Research Associates (ERA) and its successors, Remington Rand

and Sperry Rand Corporation. Engineering Research Associates was a pioneering computer firm started in 1946 by a small group that included William Norris. Cray involved himself in circuit, logic, and software design, a collection of subjects that few could do all at once. He designed the ERA 1101, one of the first scientific machines. He was the main designer on the Univac 1103 computer.

In 1957 Cray, along with William Norris and seven others, left Sperry Rand Corporation to start a new company, Control Data Corporation (CDC). Tremendous number-crunching capabilities are required to process scientific data. Cray was determined to build superfast and superpowerful computers to meet these needs. Cray convinced the company president, William Norris, to build such equipment. The computers could be sold to aircraft firms, universities, and the Department of Defense. Such clients did not need heavy investment in support or marketing and they could do their own programming. Cray's first project, the CDC 1604 computer, was so successful in the scientific community that CDC built a private laboratory for Cray in his hometown. The laboratory was within walking distance of Cray's house. The CDC 6600 computer followed five years later. This was the most powerful computer of its time. The CDC 6600 was the first computer to employ a freon cooling system, to prevent the densely packed components (the CDC 6600 had 350,000 transistors) from overheating. But it was not until the 1969 introduction of the CDC 7600, considered by many to be the first supercomputer, that Cray found his computing niche. Later, Cray designed the CDC 8600, but CDC chose not to market it.

Cray left CDC in 1972 to set up Cray Research Inc. with $500,000 in startup money from CDC. Cray insisted that the new firm would build them one at a time. Cray Research had become the dominant force in supercomputers by the late 1970s.

The first CRAY-1 supercomputer made its debut in 1976 at Los Alamos National Laboratories. The CRAY-1 was unique; it was the first practical and effective example of vector processing, in which the computer works on many different parts of the problem at once. This high-speed parallel processing is meant to increase processing rates.

Three years after the debut of the CRAY-1, Cray Research announced the decision to build the CRAY-2, which was to have six to twelve times as much power as the CRAY-1. The first production model was released in 1985. It had the largest internal memory capacity of any computer—2 billion bytes and a speed of 1.2 billion floating-point operations per second.

By early 1985, Cray was working on a follow-up to the CRAY-2, to be called the CRAY-3. This computer has an 8-billion-byte memory and is five to ten times faster than its predecessor.

Seymour Cray is the man who put the speed and the "super" into the supercomputer. Without his systems, what now takes seconds to solve would have required months, maybe even years. He received the IEEE Engineering Leadership Recognition "for exceptional personal leadership in the design and construction of the world's highest performance general-purpose supercomputers."

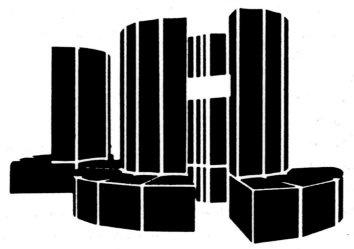

The first supercomputer (CRAY-1) was designed by Seymour Cray at Cray Research, Inc. It was the first practical and effective example of vector processing, in which the comptuer works on many different parts of the problem at once. This high-speed parallel processing is meant to increase processing rates.

Steven Jobs and Stephen Wozniak formed Apple Computer, Inc. and introduced the Apple II microcomputer. The Apple II was easy to use and became known as the Volkswagen of computers.

STEVEN JOBS

born 1955

Steven Paul Jobs was born on February 24, 1955, orphaned, and raised by adoptive parents, Paul and Clara Jobs. Steve's adopted father was a machinist at Spectra-Physics. When Steve was five, he moved with his parents to Palo Alto, California, because his father had been transferred. It was from his father that Steve acquired his first interest in mechanical things and electronics.

Steve was twelve when he saw his first computer at Hewlett-Packard. The company had invited a group of schoolchildren to the plant for lectures and some hands-on practice. The experience left

Jobs in awe of the device and he wanted one of his own. Several months later, Steve phoned directly to William Hewlett, co-founder of Hewlett-Packard, to ask for some help in building a frequency counter, a device used to measure the speed of electronic impulses, for a school project. Hewlett provided Steve with some parts. He also offered him a job for the summer after his high school freshman year, putting screws in frequency counters at Hewlett-Packard.

Steve Jobs was sixteen when he met his eventual business partner, Stephen Wozniak, then twenty-one. Both had a gift for putting technology to lighthearted uses. One idea they marketed was a "blue box" that permitted its users to make long-distance telephone calls free. They sold about two hundred boxes and then stopped producing them, as it bordered on the illegal. Jobs further developed his business skills in high school, fixing stereos and selling them to classmates.

In 1972, Jobs graduated from Homestead High School in Cupertino, California. That fall he went to Reed College in Portland, Oregon, but dropped out during the second semester. He stayed around campus for another year, attending classes occasionally and reading a good deal about Eastern religions. He left Reed College for good in early 1974. He then returned home and got a job as a video game designer for Atari. Jobs worked at night, and Wozniak often came by to play with the company's video games.

The introduction of the Altair microcomputer had led to the formation of computer clubs all over the country. The turning point in Job's life came when he began dropping by the Homebrew Computer Club, an organization of computer enthusiasts in Silicon Valley. Wozniak, a founding member of Homebrew, had been designing calculators at Hewlett-Packard during this time.

In 1975, Wozniak and Jobs started building, their own microprocessor-based computer. They used an 8-bit 6502 microprocessor designed by MOS Technology. The computer consisted of only a printed circuit board without a keyboard, case,

memory, or power supply. It could, however, be used for developing programs, playing games, and running BASIC language programs. The computer was called the Apple I. Jobs and Wozniak set up a partnership, Apple Computer, Inc., to market the product. All told, they sold about 175 Apple I computers for $500 each, netting about half that sum in profit. (The retail price of the Apple I was $666.66.)

In 1977, Jobs and Wozniak went on to develop a more sophisticated computer, the elegant-looking Apple II. This computer had a sleek, lightweight, beige plastic case; the keyboard and computer merged in a modular design. The $1,350 Apple II weighed twelve pounds and was easy to use. It became known as the Volkswagen of computers. Two milestones in Apple history are especially noteworthy. One was the announcement in the summer of 1978 of the availability of a disk drive, which provided faster, more efficient access to the computer's memory. The second milestone was the arrival of the spreadsheet program called VisiCalc. It was at first available exclusively on Apple II computers, beginning in October 1979, and sold for only $100. By September 1980, more than 130,000 Apple II computers had been sold. By the end of 1983, six years after its incorporation, Apple Computer had almost 4,700 employees and $983 million in sales.

In January 1984, Apple Computer announced the Macintosh computer. This was Steve Job's electronic baby. He shaped it, nourished it, and pampered it into life. Working on the Macintosh project was the most exciting and absorbing thing Jobs had ever done. The Macintosh became one of the most exciting and easy-to-use computers of all time.

In September 1985, after a management disagreement with Apple president John Sculley, Jobs resigned as chairman of Apple Computer. He established a new firm, called NeXT, Inc. His plan was to market a sophisticated "scholar's workstation" for under $10,000 to universities and colleges.

In 1988, after three years of secretive designing and building, Jobs unveiled the NeXT computer system. The machine, which sold for $6,500, was so sophisticated it could animate almost lifelike three-dimensional images. It was as easy to use as a personal computer, but as powerful as workstations used by scientists and engineers that cost twice as much. The NeXT system was never successful and was discontinued in the early 1990s.

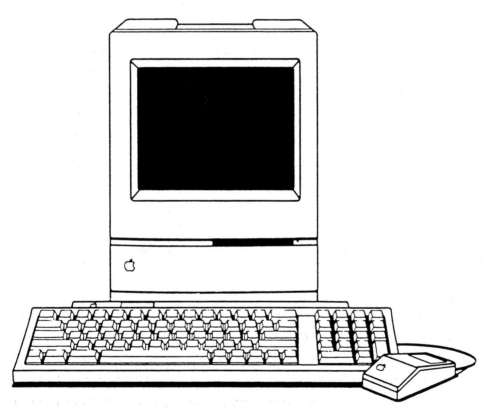

In 1984, Steven Jobs and Apple Computer, Inc. introduced the Apple Macintosh microcomputer to the world. Jobs shaped this machine, nourished it, and pampered it into life. The Macintosh became one of the most exciting and easy-to-use computers of all time.

STEPHEN WOZNIAK

born 1950

Stephen G. Wozniak was born in 1950. He was the son of an engineer; his father, Francis, helped design satellite guidance systems at the Lockheed Missiles & Space Company plant in Sunnyvale, California, not far from Intel and Fairchild Semiconductor. Francis taught his son the fundamentals of electronics and encouraged him to experiment on his own. Woz, as Stephen was known to his friends, became an avid electronics hobbyist. He had a talent for electronics, and he built all sorts of gadgets, including a transistor radio. By the time he was in the sixth grade, he had decided to become an electronics engineer.

Woz was bored by school. He shone in the few classes that interested him, mathematics and science, and did poorly in the rest. Electronics and computers were his greatest interests, and neither his junior high school nor his high school had much to offer him in either subject. He took to reading computer manuals and programming textbooks on his own, and he soon pulled ahead of his fellow students and even his teachers. When he was thirteen, he built a transistorized calculator that won first prize in a Bay Area science fair. He was drawn to minicomputers most of all, admiring their compactness, accessibility, and inexpensiveness. By the end of high school, Woz knew that he wanted to become a computer engineer. Woz graduated from Homestead High School in Cupertino, California.

Woz attended the University of Colorado for one year and later transferred to De Anza College, a junior college in Cupertino. He later left school altogether and worked for a year as a programmer for a small computer company. In 1971, he tried college again at the University of California at Berkeley. That did not last long and he dropped out and went to work as an engineer in the calculator division of Hewlett-Packard Company in Palo Alto, California.

In the summer of 1971, a friend introduced him to a quiet, intense, long-haired teenager by the name of Steven Jobs. Jobs, who was sixteen years old at the time, was an electronic hobbyist as well as a student at Homestead High School, Woz's alma mater.

The introduction of the Altair microcomputer had led to the information of computer clubs all over the country, including one in Silicon Valley known as the Homebrew Computer Club. Woz was a founding member of this club and was one of the most active members. Steve Jobs also attended meetings at the Homebrew Computer Club.

In 1975, Jobs and Woz bought a $25 microprocessor and built a computer in the living room of Jobs' parents' house in Palo Alto.

Although it was not as powerful as other available computers, it was cheaper and less complicated, and it included circuits that enabled it to be connected directly to a display monitor. Woz did most of the work, but Jobs, who was trying to persuade Woz to go into business with him, chipped in with many suggestions. The computer was called the Apple I. Jobs and Woz set up a partnership, Apple Computer, Inc., to market the computer.

In 1977, Jobs and Woz went on to develop a more sophisticated computer, the elegant-looking Apple II. By late 1980, more than 130,000 Apple II computers had been sold. By the end of 1983 Apple Computer had almost 4,700 employees and $983 million in sales. Today Apple Computer is a multibillion-dollar business.

Wozniak, who was always more interested in engineering than management, took leave from Apple Computer to pursue other things, such as earning a computer science degree under an alias from the University of California in the early 1980s. In 1985, he left Apple Computer to start a company called CL9 (as in "cloud nine"). Here he designed an infrared remote control device that can operate any component of a home entertainment system, from television to VCR, regardless of the manufacturers.

Stephen Wozniak at the keyboard of an Apple Macintosh microcomputer.

PROGRESS IN PROGRAMMING

There are more than 1000 different programming languages used by programers to tell a computer what to do. While some languages have stood the test of time, others were developed and used for a particular computer system and then disappeared. Each model of a computer must have its own language translator because a computer can only understand its own unique machine language. Usually the computer's language translator, called a compiler, assembler, or interpreter, is obtained from the manufacturer of the computer.

A program written in a programming language such as BASIC, Pascal or COBOL must be translated into machine language commands before the program can be used to process data.

Pioneers, computer scientists, entrepreneurs; the following people made major contributions to the development of programming languages and software systems: Augusta Ada Byron, who was the world's first programmer; Grace Murray Hopper, who developed several early programming languages; Edsger W. Dijkstra, who influenced the art of computer programming; John G. Kemeny and Thomas E. Kurtz, who developed BASIC, the most popular programming language; William H. Gates, who built Microsoft Corporation, a programing empire; and Daniel Bricklin, who developed VisiCalc, the first electronic spreadsheet.

AUGUSTA ADA BYRON

1815-1852

Augusta Ada Byron was born in London on December 10, 1815, to George Gordon Byron, better known as Lord Byron, and Anne Isabella Milbanke Byron. Anne and Lord Byron separated a little over a month after the birth of their daughter; Lord Byron then left England, never to return. Ada, as she was known in the family circle, married William, eighth Lord King, in 1835, and three years later became known as the Countess of Lovelace.

"I hope that the gods have made her anything save *poetical*— it is enough to have one such fool in a family." The comment came from the pen of Lord Byron. The great English poet and ladies' man was referring to his only legitimate daughter, seven-year-old Ada, and the time was 1823, the year before his death, at thirty-six.

Ada was well tutored by those around her (British logician Augustus De Morgan was a close family friend), but she hungered for more knowledge than they could provide. She was actively seeking a mentor when Charles Babbage, the noted English mathematician and inventor, came to the house to demonstrate his Difference Engine for her mother's friends. Then and there, Ada resolved to help him realize his grandest dream: the long-planned but never constructed Analytical Engine. Present on that historic evening was Mrs. De Morgan, who wrote in her memoirs: "While the rest of the party gazed at this beautiful instrument with the same sort of expression and feeling that some savages are said to have shown on first seeing a looking glass or hearing a gun, Miss Byron, young as she was, understood its workings and saw the great beauty of the invention."

Ada and Babbage became close friends, writing to each other regularly on topics that ranged from the design of machine tools to the latest society gossip. There is little doubt from these letters that Babbage was rather in love with the beautiful young countess whose mind so closely matched his own. Ada, however, was only in love with Babbage's Analytical Engine.

The Analytical Engine was what we would now call a programmable computer, with an almost infinite capacity for changes in its program. The machine, which depended on the interaction of hundreds of accurately machined gear wheels, was never actually built; however, this did not prevent Ada and Babbage from establishing the procedures for how the machine would work when it was finally completed.

General Luigi Menabrea, a celebrated Italian engineer and general, was shown the prototype of the Analytical Engine. On returning to Italy, he wrote a technical account of the machine in

French. Ada, while preparing an English translation of this publication, added many footnotes and appendices. This translated paper, the only one of Ada's that was saved, was the best description of the computer that was to be written for almost a hundred years. It was through Ada's writings that the understanding of the Analytical Engine was preserved into the twentieth century.

She also had the idea that she and Babbage, surely the most distinguished mathematicians of their generation, could create a scheme to calculate the odds on horse races, the profits to go to the development of Babbage's Analytical Engine. In her effort to develop a mathematically infallible system for betting on the ponies, she had to pawn her husband's family jewels twice to pay off blackmailing bookies.

By preparing the instructions needed to carry out computations on Babbage's calculator, Ada became the world's first computer programmer. The U.S. Pentagon has honored Ada Byron by naming a computer language after her—Ada. This language, which is similar to the language Pascal, is designed to be used on Department of Defense systems. Ada is now a registered trademark of the U.S. Department of Defense.

On November 27, 1852, at the age of thirty-six, the exact age at which her father, Lord Byron, had died, Ada died of cancer. She was buried in the Byron vault at Hucknall Torkard church in Nottinghamshire. At her own wish, she lies at the side of her father.

> *Lady Lovelace (Augusta Ada Byron) was the daughter of Lord Byron and one of the most beautiful programmers that ever lived.*
>
> Lord Bowden

Augusta Ada Byron, Countess of Lovelace, is generally credited as being the first programmer, and is the namesake of the programming language Ada. She was familiar with Charles Babbage's work and helped to document and clarify some of his efforts. She had considerable mathematical talent and developed several programs for performing mathematical calculations on the Analytical Engine.

GRACE HOPPER

1906-1992

Grace Brewster Murray Hopper was born on December 9, 1906, in New York. She earned her bachelor of arts degree in 1928 at Vassar College, where she was elected to Phi Beta Kappa. She did graduate work at Yale University receiving both her masters (1930) and doctoral (1934) degrees in mathematics. Her dissertation, entitled "New Types of Irreducibility Criteria," was written under the supervision of the algebraist Oystein Ore.

Hopper returned to Vassar as an assistant in mathematics in 1931, becoming, successively, instructor, assistant professor, and associate professor. In December 1943, she entered the U.S. Naval Reserve, was commissioned Lieutenant (JG), and ordered to the Bureau of Ordnance Computation Project at Harvard University. Here she learned to program the Mark I computer.

In 1946, she resigned from her leave-of-absence from Vassar and joined the Harvard Faculty as a Research Fellow in Engineering Sciences and Applied Physics at the Computation Laboratory, where work continued on the Mark II and Mark III computers for the Navy.

In 1949, Hopper joined, as senior mathematician, the Eckert-Mauchly Computer Corporation in Philadelphia, then building the Univac I, the first commercial large-scale electronic computer. She remained with the company as a senior programmer when it was bought by Remington Rand (later to become Sperry Rand Corporation, Sperry Corporation, and Unisys Corporation). There she pioneered in the development of the COBOL compiler and later became one of the prime movers in the development of COBOL programming language in the 1950s. The Common Business Oriented Language (COBOL) was based on Hopper's FLOMATIC, the first English-language data processing language. Her reason for developing the business compiler was, simply, why start from scratch with every program you write when a compiler could be developed to do much of the basic work for you over and over again.

Throughout her business life, Hopper was affectionately anchored to the Navy. She chose to retire in 1966, but the Navy called her back to active duty a year later, when she was sixty. She finally left the fleet with the rank of Rear Admiral in 1986 at the age of seventy-nine. Grace Hopper was one of the U.S. Navy's greatest public relations assets. She traveled widely, speaking about computers on the Navy's behalf, exhibiting an honest pride in the Navy and her country, and talking vividly and forthrightly about the work she loved. She encouraged people to be innovative. One of her favorite pieces of advice was, "It is easier to apologize than to get permission."

In her lectures, Hopper lashed out at the computer industry on several counts. Its lack of standards—for programming languages, computer architecture, data structure, and networks—was costing the government hundreds of millions of dollars a year in hardware and software that had to be thrown out because of incompatibility.

Hopper also condemned the notion that larger computers were automatically superior. As an analogy, she pointed out that when a farmer had to move a big, heavy boulder, and one of his oxen was not strong enough to do the job alone, he did not try to raise a bigger ox. He added another ox. Likewise, large volumes of data were better handled by multiple users than by a larger machine.

On September 1, 1986, just over two weeks after she retired from the Navy, she began working as a roving speaker for Digital Equipment Corporation.

Hopper's achievements in the design and preparation of problem solutions for digital computers distinguished her as one of the major contributors to program development throughout a period spanning three computer generations. She disseminated her thoughts and ideas not only through her writings, but also through numerous lecture tours.

"Amazing Grace" Hopper died on New Year's Day, 1992. She was eighty-five.

Grace Hopper is often thought of as the grandmother of COBOL.

Rear Admiral Grace Hopper is best known for the development of computer programming languages that simplified the human interface with computer technology. She was awarded the National Medal of Technology by President Bush in 1991.

EDSGER DIJKSTRA

born 1930

Edsger W. Dijkstra was born in the Netherlands in 1930. He entered the programming profession in 1952, programmed computers for three years, and then decided to help make programming a respectable discipline in the years to come. He was aware that automatic computers were here to stay.

Dijkstra worked in theoretical physics, algorithm design, compiler construction, process synchronization, operating system design, programming language semantics, programming methodology, and mathematical methodology in general, such as the design of adequate notations and the exploitation of proof theory to guide the design of streamlined formal arguments.

The working vocabulary of programmers everywhere is studded with words originated or forcefully promulgated by Dijkstra: display, sempahore, deadly embrace, go-to-less programming, structured programming.

Dijkstra has had a strong influence on programming. He has introduced a special style: his approach to programming as a high, intellectual challenge; his eloquent insistence and practical demonstration that programs should be composed correctly, not just debugged into correctness; and his illuminating perception of problems at the foundations of program design.

He has published many papers, both technical and reflective, among which are especially to be noted his already classic papers on cooperating sequential processes, his indictment of the go-to statement, and his philosophical addresses at the IFIP Congresses in 1962 and 1965. An influential series of letters by Dijkstra were published on the art of composing programs.

Dijkstra was presented the 1972 Association for Computing Machinery (ACM) Turing Award in recognition of his outstanding contributions to the programming field. The Turing Award, the Associations's highest recognition of technical contributions to the computing community, honors Alan M. Turing, the English mathematician who defined the computer prototype Turing machine and helped break German ciphers during World War II. In his Turing lecture at the 1972 ACM Annual Conference, Dijkstra remarked: "We shall do a much better programming job, provided that we approach the task with a full appreciation of its tremendous difficulty, provided that we respect the intrinsic limitations of the human mind and approach the task as very humble programmers."

As of 1991, Dijkstra occupied the Schlumberger Centennial Chair in Computer Science and was a professor of mathematics, both at the University of Texas at Austin.

JOHN KEMENY

1926-1992

John George Kemeny, co-designer of the BASIC programming language, was born in Budapest, Hungary, on May 31, 1926. Kemeny's father believed that Hitler's march into Vienna in early 1938 augured worse things, so he left on his own for the United States. A year and a half later, in early 1940, he sent for his wife, daughter, and teen-aged son, John. The family sailed to America without incident. Kemeny attended school in New York City. In 1943, he entered Princeton University, where he studied mathematics.

In 1945, during his junior year at Princeton, he was drafted and sent to Los Alamos, New Mexico, where organizers of the Manhattan Project had undertaken a crash program to accelerate development of the atom bomb. Here he worked in the project's computing center (using IBM bookkeeping calculators) solving mathematical problems.

After the war he retuned to Princeton, where he received a doctoral degree in mathematics. While completing his dissertation, he served as Albert Einstein's research assistant at the Institute for Advanced Study. Einstein always had a mathematician as a research assistant. Kemeny worked three or four days a week with Einstein, who at the time was completing his work on unified field theory. Kemeny spent a considerable amount of time checking Einstein's calculations.

Kemeny taught mathematics for two years and philosophy for another two years at Princeton. In 1953, he started teaching mathematics and philosophy at Dartmouth College. He served as chairman of the mathematics department from 1956 to 1968 and as president of the college from 1970 to 1981.

At 4:00 a.m. on May 1, 1964, the first BASIC program ran on a General Electric Company time-sharing system. Kemeny, along with Thomas Kurtz, was responsible for this major event in computing history. The time-sharing concept, pioneered by Fernando Corbato and John McCarthy at MIT, would enable a new breed of users to have better access to, and quicker turnaround time on, the computers of the day. The Dartmouth Time-Sharing System was very popular with students who became computer literate almost overnight. What those novice users needed next was a user-friendly language to make real use of that newfound literacy. The Beginner's All-Purpose Symbolic Instruction Code (BASIC), developed by Kemeny and Kurtz, was the solution to this problem. BASIC, which eased the process of developing and debugging programs, soon became the most popular programming language for beginners.

In 1985, Kemeny and Kurtz developed True BASIC, a more powerful version of their legendary language. Kemeny wrote *A Philosopher Looks At Science* and *Man and the Computer: A New Symbiosis*. He co-authored thirteen books, including *Basic Programming*. He received more than seventy honorary degrees and awards, including the Institute of Electrical and Electronic Engineers Computer Pioneer Medal in 1986 and the IBM Louis Robinson Award in 1990.

Kemeny died very unexpectedly on December 26, 1992, at the age of sixty-six.

> *The man ignorant of mathematics will be increasingly limited in his grasp of the main forces of civilization.*
>
> John Kemeny

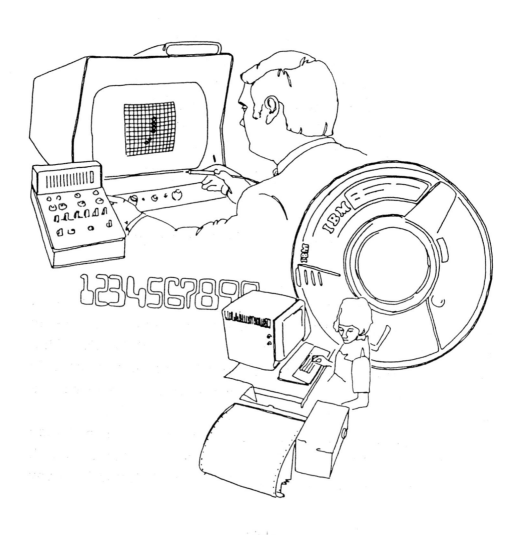

THOMAS KURTZ

born 1928

Thomas E. Kurtz, co-designer of the BASIC programming language, was born on February 22, 1928, in Oak Park, Illinois. In 1950 he graduated from Knox College in Galesburt, Illinois, with a degree in mathematics. Kurtz received a doctoral degree in mathematics from Princeton University in 1956. His thesis was on a problem of multiple comparisons in mathematical statistics.

Kurtz joined the Dartmouth College faculty in 1956 and began teaching mathematics. Almost immediately he became involved with computers. In his first year, he traveled to General Electric Company in Lynn, Massachusetts, to use their computers. For the following two years, he used an IBM 704 computer at MIT.

In the early 1960s Kurtz and John Kemeny designed the BASIC programming language. Their goal was to develop a simple and powerful programming language that students of all disciplines could learn easily. The result was Beginner's All-Purpose Symbolic Instruction Code (BASIC). BASIC is the most common programming language used on computers today. Kurtz and Kemeny tried to impress on members of the college and university community the philosophy that an understanding of computers is as necessary to life as being able to read and write, and that computers should be as accessible as a library. At Dartmouth College, all students can use the library computers at little or no cost. This philosophy is now being implemented in other colleges and universities throughout America.

Kurtz is the co-author (with Kemeny) of one of the original BASIC books (*BASIC Programming*, Dartmouth College, Dartmouth, N.H., 1969). Kurtz has been a member of the President's Science Advisory Commission (1965-1966) and Director of Dartmouth's Kiewit Computation Center and Director of the Office of Academic Computing at Dartmouth.

In the summer of 1983, Kurtz and Kemeny started work on an improved version of the BASIC programming language. Their new language, called True BASIC, was introduced on March 5, 1985. A more powerful language than BASIC, it incorporates interactive graphics, a window manager, formatting tools, and a high-level debugger. It has an interface and command structure that are identical regardless of what computer is being used; this was meant to overcome problems that arose with the original BASIC, requiring different versions for different computers.

NIKLAUS WIRTH

Niklaus Wirth entered the computing field in 1960. He received his doctoral degree from the University of California at Berkeley in 1963 and was assistant professor at Stanford University until 1967. He was a professor at the Swiss Federal Institute of Technology (ETH) in Zurich from 1968 to 1984. From 1982 to 1984 he was chairman of the division of computer science (Informatik) at ETH.

His first introduction to computers and programming was a course in numerical analysis at Laval University in Canada. Here, however, the Alvac IIIE computer was out of order most of the time, and exercises in programming remained on paper in the form of untested sequences of hexadecimal codes. His next attempt at using computers was with the Bendix G-15 computer. This machine required the user to allocate program instructions cleverly on the drum. If the user did not, the programs could well run slower by a factor of 100. It was obvious to Wirth that computers of the future had to be more effectively programmable. Wirth therefore gave up the idea of studying how to design hardware in favor of studying how to use it more elegantly.

He joined a research group that was engaged in the development of a compiler and its use on an IBM 704. The language was called NELIAC, a dialect of Algol 58. The benefits of such a "language" were quickly obvious, and the task of automatically translating programs into machine code posed challenging problems. The NELIAC compiler, itself written in NELIAC, was an intricate mess. Wirth felt that programs should be designed according to the same principles as electronic circuits, that is, clearly subdivided into parts with only a few wires going across the boundaries. Only by understanding one part at a time would there be hope of finally understanding the whole. Algol 60 was the first language defined with clarity; its syntax was even specified in a rigorous formalism. Could Algol's principles be condensed and crystallized even further?

Wirth then started his adventures in programming languages. The first experiment led to the development of EULER, an Algol-like programming language. This language created a basis for the systematic design of compilers. The next language developed by Wirth was Algol W. This language took Algol 60 as a starting point and attempted to rectify some of the ambiguities and deficiencies of the language.

In the fall of 1967, Wirth returned to Switzerland. A year later he was able to implement the language that later became known as Pascal. After an extensive development phase, a Pascal compiler became operational in 1970. The development of Pascal was based

156

on two principal aims. The first was to make available a language suitable to teach programming as a systematic discipline based on certain fundamental concepts clearly and naturally reflected by the language. The second was to develop implementations of the language that are both reliable and efficient on available computers. Pascal has become a very popular teaching language because it allows the teacher to concentrate more heavily on structures and concepts than features and peculiarities.

Wirth's ability in language design is complemented by an excellent writing ability. In 1971, Wirth published a paper on structured programming that recommended top-down structuring of programs (i.e., successively refining program stubs until the program is fully elaborated). Two later papers on real-time programming and notation speak to Wirth's consistent and dedicated search for an adequate language formalism.

As Pascal was gaining widespread recognition throughout the world, Wirth was investigating the subject of multiprogramming. The attempt to distill concrete rules for a multiprogramming discipline led Wirth to formulate them in terms of a small set of programming facilities. The result was the programming language Modula-2 Although a Pascal-like language, Modula-2 provides two features lacking in Pascal: easy hardware access and separate compilation of program modules.

In 1980, Wirth blended the Pascal and Modula-2 languages to form the native language of LILITH, a workstation dedicated specifically to software design. The LILITH project proved that it is not only possible but advantageous to design a single-language system. Everything from device drivers to text and graphics editors is written in the same language. There is not distinction between modules belonging to the operating system and those belonging to the user's program.

The hallmarks of a programming language designed by Wirth are its simplicity, economy of design, and high-quality engineering, which result in a language whose notation appears to be a natural extension of algorithmic thinking rather than an extraneous formalism.

Modula-2 (programming language) grew out of Pascal and incorporates a few major and some minor improvements.

Niklaus Wirth

Someone asked Niklaus Wirth how he pronounced his name. He is reported to have said, *"You can call me by name or you can call me by value. If you call me by name it is 'VIRT.' If you call me by value, it is 'WORTH.'"*

Niklaus Wirth

About Pascal—*"In the interest of increased quality of software products, we may be well advised to get rid of many facilities of modern, baroque programming languages that are widely advertised in the name of 'user-orientation,' 'scientific sophistication,' and 'progress.'"*

Niklaus Wirth

WILLIAM GATES

born 1955

William H. Gates was born in Seattle, Washington, on October 28, 1955. His father is a prominent a lawyer and his mother has served on numerous corporate, charitable, and civil boards. He taught himself programming at age thirteen, having taken up computer studies in 1967 as a seventh-grader at the private Lakeside School in Seattle. Gates and a ninth-grader named Paul Allen were enthralled about using the school's time-shared computer. Gates and Allen's enthusiasm has not waned since. In the late 1960s, Gates and some other Seattle teenagers would ride their bicycles each afternoon to the Computer Center Corporation office, where they searched for errors in the programs being run on the Center's computer. They eventually went on the firm's payroll. Throughout their high school years, Gates and Allen worked as programming consultants.

TRW, a large software firm in Vancouver, Washington, offered Gates and Allen $20,000 a year, each, to work in a software development group. Gates took a year-long leave from high school during his senior year to go to work for TRW. When work diminished, he entered Harvard University. He was planning to stay away from computers. Allen went to work as a systems programmer for Honeywell, near Boston.

Gates entered Harvard in the fall of 1973. Allen happened to be strolling through Harvard Square one day when he noticed the January issue of *Popular Electronics* on a news stand. Allen bought a copy and went on to visit Gates. The Altair microcomputer, based on the Intel 8080 chip, made by an Albuquerque, New Mexico, firm called MITS, and selling for $350, appeared on the cover. Here was the first truly cheap computer! To anyone who knew computers then, it was instantly clear that the Altair required, more than anything else, a BASIC interpreter, to permit users to write programs in a high-level language rather than in machine code. Allen proposed to Gates that the two try to write a BASIC interpreter for the Altair. Gates and Allen phoned Edward Roberts, the MITS founder who had built the Altair, with an offer to write a BASIC interpreter for the Altair. Roberts was interested, and the pair started working. Allen and Gates spent February and March of 1975 working in Gates' small dormitory room at Harvard. Allen flew out to Albuquerque to demonstrate the interpreter. Roberts bought it and Gates and Allen had created an industry standard, one that would hold the field for the next six years.

Allen promptly became MITS' software director. Gates dropped out of Harvard at the end of his sophomore year in 1975 and went to work as a free-lance software writer. It was then that Gates and Allen formed Microsoft Corporation. Within eighteen months, the two had made a few hundred thousand dollars for their new firm. They were writing programs for Apple Computer, Inc. and Commodore. During the first year, Gates and Allen expanded BASIC so that it would run on other microcomputers.

In 1980, IBM asked Gates to design the operating system for their new machine, what would become the incredibly popular IBM PC. In early 1981, Gates delivered the operating system that would control the IBM PC. Microsoft Disk Operating System (MS-DOS) very quickly became the major operating system for personal computers in the United States. Over two million copies of MS-DOS had been sold as of the spring of 1984.

Other companies turned to Gates as well. Apple Computer, Inc. asked him to develop software for the Macintosh computer. He helped design the Radio Shack Model 100. Beginning in the mid-1980s, Microsoft Corporation started developing applications software, including Microsoft Word, for word processing; Microsoft Works, for business applications; and Flight Simulator, which permits someone to sit at a computer and simulate the piloting of a plane.

In 1982, Gates dreamed of a piece of software, called Windows, that he hoped would push his company to the top of the personal computer software industry. The product was developed, and on April 2, 1987, IBM chose Windows as a key piece of software for their new generation of personal computers—IBM PS/2. Windows is built into the operating system—the software that controls a computer's basic functions and runs applications software such as spreadsheets, word processors, and database managers. Windows, which uses graphics similar to those of Apple Computer's Macintosh computer, makes IBM PCs much easier to use by simplifying the commands needed to operate them. In 1995, Microsoft released Windows 95, an upgraded version of the operating system for IBM-compatible computers.

Microsoft Corporation has set standards for the software industry in languages, operating systems, and application software.

Gates has provided the vision for the company's new product ideas and technologies.

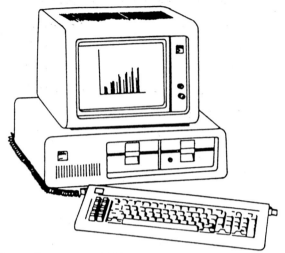

In 1981, William Gates and Microsoft Corporation delivered to IBM the operating system that would control the IBM PC. MS-DOS quickly became the major operating system for IBM-compatible computers.

It's exciting to be involved in building tools that I think can make jobs a lot more interesting. I think this information age is a good thing. I think it's empowering to the individual. I think it makes the world a richer place.

William Gates

Software is a great combination between artistry and engineering. When you finally get done and get to appreciate what you have, it is like a part of yourself that you've put together.

William Gates

162

DANIEL BRICKLIN

born 1951

Daniel Bricklin was born in Philadelphia, Pennsylvania, on July 16, 1951. He grew up there, attending Solomon Schechter Day School. In 1969, he enrolled at the Massachusetts Institute of Technology (MIT) and began studying mathematics, switching in the middle of his junior year to computer science. Bricklin graduated from MIT in 1973 with a bachelor of science degree in electrical engineering and computer science. While at MIT, he worked a great deal with a graduate student named Bob Frankston. The two agreed they would go into business together one day.

Bricklin wanted to stay close to computers, so in the fall of 1973, he started working for Digital Equipment Corporation (DEC) near Boston. His first task there was to program a wire-service interface to a newspaper typesetting system. He also worked on computerized typesetting and obtained much experience with visual display screens and editing. His most important job at DEC was as project leader of the company's first word processing system, WPS-8, one of the earliest word processing programs. Bricklin wrote a large part of the program's code, as well as the functional specifications.

In 1976, he became a senior systems programmer for Fas Fax Corporation, manufacturers of electronic cash registers. While here, he worked closely with the firm's hardware designers and learned something about running a small business. He left there in 1977 and that fall entered graduate school in business at Harvard University.

Bricklin wanted to start a small business and, while at Harvard, he hoped to learn the "secrets" of doing this. There was a great deal of time to daydream in his classes. One day in the spring of 1978, he came up with the idea of the electronic spreadsheet. He imagined the electronic calculator, the word processor that would work with numbers. Could not a small computer speed up the calculations required in solving business problems? Bricklin was a programmer who wanted to apply his programming skills to creating a kind of electronic blackboard that would perform calculations automatically.

Bricklin and Frankston got together and decided they would work on an electronic spreadsheet in Fankston's attic in Arlington, Massachusetts. One of the most difficult and important ideas was how to label where something was. Bricklin decided that the simplest way was to use a grid coordinate system. As people usually think in letters and numbers, he labeled the top with letters and put numbers down the side. Bricklin used his experience working with interpreters to view VisiCalc as a programming language.

In the fall of 1978, Bricklin and Frankson made a deal with Dan Fylstra that they would produce this electronic spreadsheet and he would publish it through his small home computer publishing company, called Personal Software (Personal Software eventually became VisiCorp). Bricklin and Frankston named their company Software Arts.

In January 1979, working versions of VisiCalc were shown to Apple Computer, Inc., Atari Corporation, and other personal computer companies. A.C. Markkula, a third owner of Apple Computer, Inc., said "Hmm, interesting checkbook program—you market it yourself, we're not interested." The first VisiCalc ad appeared in the May 1979 issue of *BYTE Magazine.*

The news of VisiCalc spread rapidly. By May 1981, VisiCalc sales had exceeded 100,000 units. In 1983, cumulative sales topped half a million units. The success of Software Arts continued until 1984 when it entered into an extended legal battle with VisiCorp over the rights to VisiCalc. In the spring of 1985, Bricklin left Software Arts to be a consultant at Lotus Corporation for a short time. In November 1985, Bricklin formed a new company, Software Garden.

> *The basic idea of what a spreadsheet would be came to me in the spring of 1978. The goal was that it had to be better than the back of an envelope.*
> Daniel Bricklin

PHOTO CREDITS

Photographs and Illustrations courtesy of: Apple Computer, Inc., pp. 128, 132, 135; Bell Laboratories, pp. 71, 72; Control Data Corporation, pp. 123, 124; Department of the Navy, p. 146; Digital Equipment Corporation, p. 113; Dover Publishing, p. 30; IBM Corporation, pp. 38, 47, 48, 76, 77, 114, 117, 119, 120; Iowa State University, pp. 82, 86; Sperry Corporation, pp. 91, 92, 95, 96, 145. All other illustrations are from the Camelot Publishing Archives.

SUGGESTED READING

For the reader who wishes to learn more about computers and the people responsible for their development, a list of references appears below:

A Computer Perspective. Charles and Ray Eames. Harvard University Press. 1973.

Ada: A Life and a Legacy. Dorothy Stein. The MIT Press. 1987.

Ada, the Enchantress of Numbers. Betty Alexandra Toole. Strawberry Press. 1992.

A Few Good Men from Univac. David E. Lundstrom. The MIT Press. 1987.

A History of Computing Technology. Michael R. Williams. Prentice Hall, Inc. 1985.

An Investigation of the Laws of Thought. George Boole. Dover Publications, Inc. 1958.

A Short History of Computers. Donald D. Spencer. Camelot Publishing Company. 1996.

Bit by Bit: An Illustrated History of Computers. Stan Angarten. Ticknor & Fields. 1984.

Breakthrough to the Computer Age. Harry Wulforst. Charles Scribner's Sons. 1982.

Charles Babbage and His Calculating Machines—Selected Writings. Philip and Emily Morrison. Dover Publications, Inc. 1961.

Charles Babbage: Father of the Computer. Dan Halacy. Crowell-Collier Press. 1970.

Charles Babbage: Pioneer of the Computer. Anthony Hyman. Princeton University Press. 1982.

Computer Facts and Firsts. Donald D. Spencer. Camelot Publishing Company. 1996.

Computer Perspectives. Maurice V. Wilkes. Morgan Kaufmann Publishers. 1995.

Computer Pioneers. J.A.N. Lee. IEEE Computer Society Press. 1995.

Computer Pioneers. Laura Greene. Franklin Watts. 1985.

Digital At Work. Jamie Parker Pearson. Digital. 1992.

Early British Computers. Simon Lavington. Digital Press. 1980.

Encyclopedia of Computer Pioneers. Donald D. Spencer. Camelot Publishing Company. 1996.

Engines of the Mind: A History of the Computer. Joel Shurkin. W.W. Norton & Company. 1984.

Famous People of Computing. Donald D. Spencer. Camelot Publishing Company. 1987.

Father Son & Co. Thomas J. Watson Jr. Bantam Books. 1990.

Gates. Stephen Manes and Paul Andrews. Doubleday. 1993.

Giant Brains: or Machines That Think. Edmund C. Berkeley. John Wiley and Sons. 1949.

Grace Hopper: Navy Admiral and Computer Pioneer. Charlene W. Billings. Enslow Publishers, Inc. 1989.

Herman Hollerith: Forgotten Giant of Information Processing. Geoffrey D. Austrian. Columbia University Press. 1982.

John von Neumann. Norman Macrae. Pantheon Books. 1992.

Landmarks in Digital Computing. Peggy A. Kidwell and Paul E. Ceruzzi. Smithsonian Institution Press. 1994.

Living with the Chip. David Manners and Tsugio Makimoto. Chapman & Hall. 1995.

Mathematics and Computers. George R. Stibitz and Jules A. Larrivee. McGraw-Hill Book Company. 1957.

Portraits in Silicon. Robert Slater. The MIT Press. 1989.

Programmers at Work. Susan Lammers. Microsoft Press. 1986.

Stretching Man's Mind: A History of Data Processing. Margaret Harmon. Mason/Charter Publishers, Inc. 1975.

The Analytical Engine. Jeremy Bernstein. Random House. 1963.

The Analytical Engine: Computers - Past, Present and Future. Jeremy Bernstein. William Morrow and Company. 1981.

The Chip. T.R. Reid. Simon and Schuster. 1984.

The Computer and the Brain. John von Neumann. Yale University Press. 1958.

The Computer Entrepreneurs. Robert Levering, Michael Katz, and Milton Moskowitz. NAL Books. 1984.

The Computer Prophets. Jerry M. Rosenberg. The Macmillan Company. 1969.

The Computer Story. Irving E. Fang. Rada Press. 1988.

The Dream Machine: Exploring The Computer Age. Jon Palfreman and Doron Swade. BBC Books. 1991.

The History of Computers. Les Freed. Ziff-Davis Press. 1995.

The History of Computing. Marguerite Zientara. CW Communications, Inc. 1981.

The Making of the Micro. Christopher Evans. Victor Gollancz Ltd. 1979.

The Microprocessor: A Biography. Michael S. Malone, Springer-Verlag. 1995.

The Origins of Digital Computers: Selected Papers. Brian Randell. Springer-Verlag. 1973.

The Story of Cybernetics. Maurice Trask. Studio Vista/Dutton Pictureback. 1971.

The Timeline of Computers. Donald D. Spencer. Camelot Publishing Company. 1996.

THINK: A Biography of the Watsons and IBM. William Rodgers. Stein and Day Publishers. 1969.

Understanding Computers, Third Edition. Donald D. Spencer. Camelot Publishing Company. 1996.

INDEX

173

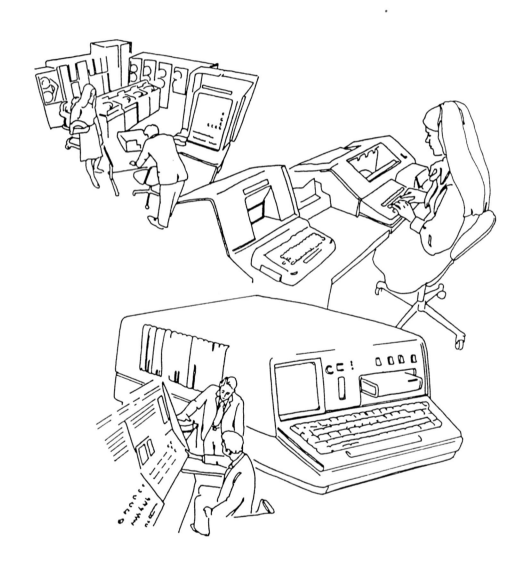